WSM

COUNTRY

INSTRUMENTALS & VOCALS

LONG-PLAYING

THE GOLDEN ERA

TWENTY CLASSIC COUNTRY TRACKS

COUNTRY
THE GOLDEN ERA

COUNTRY
THE GOLDEN ERA

MICHAEL HEATLEY

CHARTWELL
BOOKS, INC.

First published in 2009 by

CHARTWELL BOOKS, INC.
A Division of
BOOK SALES, INC.
276 Fifth Avenue Suite 206
New York, New York 10001

ISBN 13: 978-0-7858-2500-5
ISBN 10: 0-7858-2500-2

Designed by
Angela Ball and Dave Ball

Project Manager
Martin Howard

All Internet site information provided was correct when provided by
the Author. The Publisher can accept no responsibility for this
information becoming incorrect.

Printed and bound in China

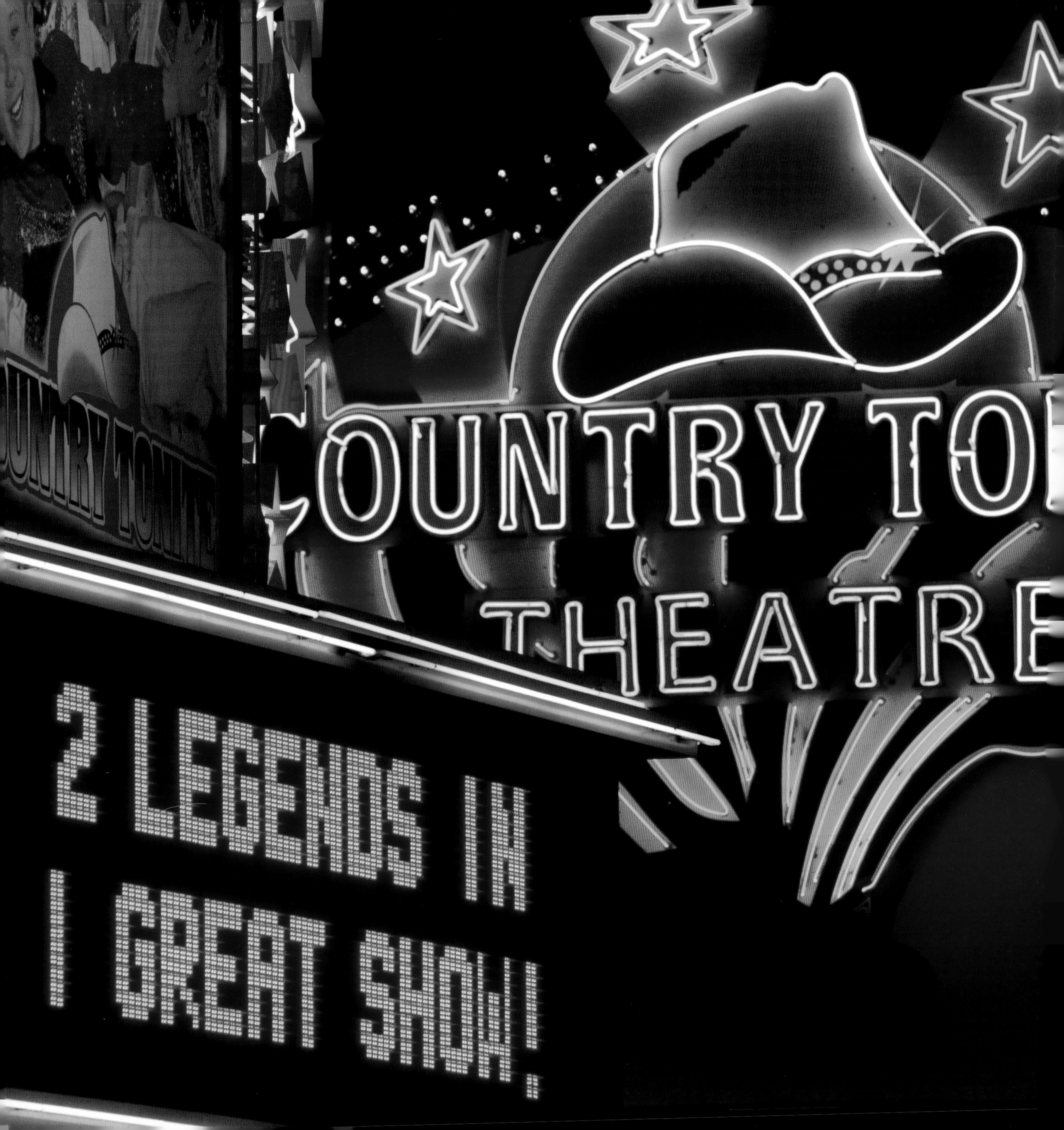

COUNTRY TONITE
COUNTRY TO
THEATRE
2 LEGENDS IN
1 GREAT SHOW!

CONTENTS

INTRODUCTION

Today's shiny, glossy conception of country music shares little, on the surface, with the rough-hewn, earthy music it emerged from. With its roots in English and Scottish folk ballads imported by early settlers, country music first stirred in the rural South where farmers and backwoodsmen handed their tales of tragedy and hardship down the generations. Finally, it emerged, with the help of radio and records, to be recognized by the wider world as an honest, powerful, and enduring musical genre in its own right. Willie Nelson probably got as near as most have done to a one-sentence description when he described country music as, "a place where people tell their life stories."

Yet while today's country is a very different proposition to its ancestor, with glossy videos, Stetsons, lipgloss, and line dancing, it retains the utmost respect for its roots. And that's the way it should be, because country music is all about tradition. As the late, great Johnny Cash put it, "If young people don't know a little about their tradition in the music they love, they really are missing their inheritance. I love to hear new stuff, but I love to hear some of the old stuff too." So a book like this, highlighting the contributions of twenty of the genre's most celebrated names from past decades remains relevant.

If respect for country is now widespread, it hasn't always been that way: who can forget *Urban Cowboy*, Hollywood's most forgettable take on country, which saw John Travolta hoping to do for Stetsons what he'd done for tight-fitting white suits in *Saturday Night Fever*? All that is now history, and even Dolly Parton who, some would say, has done country a disservice with her "caricatured"

Above: The record label of Hill Billie Blues by Uncle Dave Macon.

style, has returned to her bluegrass roots with great success. "I had to get rich in order to sing like I'm poor again." she's said, commenting on the risk of losing her "pop" audience.

The first ever collection of cowboy songs was published in 1908. Musicologist John Lomax followed up two years later with "Cowboy Songs And Other Frontier Ballads," and interest in white musical heritage was increased still further by folk archivist Cecil Sharp's publishing of songs from the Appalachian mountains from 1917 onward. The seeds of country had been well and truly sown.

Popular music in the 1920s fell into two categories: race (or black) music and its white counterpart, hillbilly music. The latter term was first coined by "Uncle" Dave Macon in his 1924 recording "Hill Billie Blues." Around this time, too, the Sears mail order catalog started offering instruments as well as songbooks and sheet music. And when a record player became a fixture in

Above: Flatt and Scruggs, front, and The Foggy Mountain Boys in 1963.

Saturday night broadcasts began in 1925, introducing the nation to many of the all-time greats of country music. WSM's signal (rated at 50,000 watts in 1934) could often be heard across the country,

The Opry began with primarily part-time artists who used the show to promote their appearances throughout the South and Midwest. But Roy Acuff, who hosted when the Grand Ole Opry made its first network broadcast on NBC in 1939 in a half-hour segment sponsored by the makers of Prince Albert Smoking Tobacco, ensured professionalism became a byword. Originally considered just another local radio show, the Opry was soon projecting the talents of Acuff and banjo-player "Uncle" Dave Macon across the South on a weekly basis and picking up an enviable listenership. This was the pre-television era, of course, and thousands of families would regularly gather round the radio to hear Nashville's "barn dances" beamed into their home.

Acuff was, of course, one of the beneficiaries of such coverage, and his "Great Speckled Bird," released in the same year the Opry debuted on the airwaves, was the first of many hit records for him. The Opry's nearest rival was the Louisiana Hayride, a radio (later television) show broadcast from the Municipal Auditorium in Shreveport, Louisiana, that, during its heyday from 1948 to 1960, also helped launch the careers of some great names.

every front room, the 78rpm shellac record made permanent what had hitherto been handed down from fathers to sons. If the blues was the music of the black working man, then country was its white counterpart.

The Victor and Okeh recording companies begin recording country artists in the early 1920s. The first pure country music recording is reckoned to be "Arkansas Traveler" and "Sallie Gooden," cut by fiddler Eck Robertson for Victor Records in 1922. Surprisingly, perhaps, this groundbreaking 78 was made in New York City. Other early landmarks were registered by Fiddlin' John Carson who recorded "Little Log Cabin in the Lane" for Okeh Records in 1923, while Vernon Dalhart's "Wreck of the Old '97"/"Lonesome Road Blues" was country's first nationwide hit in 1924. "Aunt" Samantha Bumgarner and Eva Davis became the first female musicians to record and release country songs in the same year.

Meanwhile, radio was the up and coming medium through which the music would spread quickest. In April 1924, WLS Radio in Chicago broadcast the first National Barn Dance, setting the scene for WSM Radio's Grand Ole Opry in Nashville, Tennessee. The Opry's live

Country's earliest instrumentation combined the banjo, introduced by African-Americans via minstrel shows, with the Scottish "fiddle"

Right: Jim Reeves poses on Country Music Jubilee, 1958.

or violin and the guitar, an instrument popular in the South from around 1910. However, as more blacks adopted the guitar, the banjo ended up being identified more closely with white music.

While radio was bringing country a wider audience, Victor Records also remained in the vanguard of country progress thanks to one man: Ralph Peer. In 1927, the musicologist discovered two landmark acts in one eventful day—The Carter Family and "Singing Brakeman" Jimmie Rodgers.

The stock market crash of 1929 heralded the Great Depression. Record sales plunged, which further increased the importance of radio. But people still needed to be entertained and in 1933 Wurlitzer introduced its first jukebox. The '30s were also to become the decade of the "Singing Cowboy," during which Hollywood projected the talents of figures like Roy Rogers, Gene Autry, and Tex Ritter. The genre originated in 1925 when Texan Carl Sprague recorded "When The Work's All Done This Fall." But it was Autry who became "America's favorite singing cowboy," scoring his first hit record, "That Silver Haired Daddy of Mine," in 1931. He was soon strumming on the big screen in a series of Westerns that promoted his music; the first, *In Old Santa Fe*, came in 1934.

Meanwhile, Western swing and honky tonk music flourished in the hands of Bob Wills and Ernest Tubb. At the height of its popularity, Western swing rivaled the popularity of big band jazz. Honky-tonk, meanwhile, was a brash brand of music that dealt with loss and disillusionment, but also celebrated the ritual of "steppin' out on a Saturday night."

Many of the pioneers who put country music on the map paid the price of hard living—Hank Williams

Right: The cover of Merle Travis' Folk Songs of the Hills album, released in 1947.

Right: Elvis Presley heads the bill on the Louisiana Hayride.

never saw his thirties, dying in the back of a limousine en route to yet another gig. With the high mortality rate and the passage of time, it's no surprise that all but a couple of our featured artists are no longer with us. Yet not all could be blamed for shining brightly and briefly. Patsy Cline's chartered plane crashed outside Nashville in 1963, while Jim Reeves suffered a similar cruel fate a year later. On the plus side, Hank Thompson and Hank Snow made it through to their eighties and enjoyed a deserved status as grand old men of country. In all cases, we have the music of all these pioneers to remember them by. And there has never been a shortage of willing torchbearers as country has risen to ever greater heights.

The electric guitar made it into the country musican's armoury thanks to Ernest Tubb, while Merle Travis, not only a major singer and songwriter, but also a much-copied instrumentalist, helped devise the solid-bodied guitar that Fender would later popularize as the Stratocaster. Travis, who was taught banjo by his musician father, adapted the style to guitar to invent "Travis Picking;" Chet Atkins was among his scholars.

After America entered the war in 1940, the Special Service Division of the U.S. military took country to a wide audience of soldiers across the world, to such an extent that Japanese troops yelled "To hell with

Above: Chet Atkins plays his guitar in Washington, D.C., 1980.

Roosevelt, to hell with Babe Ruth, to hell with Roy Acuff," as they charged the beaches at Okinawa. Back home, country's profile was growing at an exponential rate. In 1942, music trade journal *Billboard* introduced a column on the music, and two years later introduced a sales chart for hillbilly songs. As the Second World War ended, Nashville, Tennessee, became the recognized center for country.

This kind of success was a beacon for the likes of Webb Pierce and Ernest Tubb. Pierce, from Louisiana, moved toward pop and rock 'n' roll by adopting the electric guitar, but greatest of all these crossover artists was, perhaps, Jim Reeves. His first album contained fiddle and steel guitar, but he soon dropped these instruments and adopted a more intimate singing style. The combination, smooth as the finest whiskey, brought his music to a far wider audience.

Alongside country, bluegrass music had originated in the 1920s from the Virginia-Tennessee border. It was fast, often instrumental "mountain music" with banjo, fiddle, and mandolin supplying the melody, backed by guitar and string bass. Derived from the string bands of the '20s it was the country equivalent of Dixieland jazz. Gospel music was also a key component in the vocal delivery. In 1947, Bill Monroe and his Blue Grass Boys recorded "Blue

Moon Of Kentucky," one of the finest examples of the bluegrass style. Two of his musicians, Lester Flatt and Earl Scruggs, left to form their own Foggy Mountain Boys and help establish bluegrass as a distinct musical style. (Over half a century later, the blockbuster film *O Brother Where Art Thou* paid its own tribute by christening the movie's fictional group the Soggy Bottom Boys.)

There are, today, many different sub-genres of country and the artists profiled in this book reflect that diversity. Ray Price and Hank Thompson, both from Texas, had one foot in Western swing and the other in honky-tonk. Canadian-born Hank Snow revived Jimmie Rodgers' yodeling style while guitarist Merle Travis' virtuoso finger-picking made his instrument simultaneously melodic and rhythmic. His 1947, album *Folk Songs Of The Hills* was highly influential.

Country songs, in which emotion generally held sway, contrasted with Tin Pan Alley's often saccharine creations. But the rewards country music now offered—at the height of his fame, Jimmie Rodgers' annual salary was said to have been over $100,000—brought more performers into the market, while increasing competition for the record-buyer's dollar ensured songwriting standards

Above: The legendary Bill Monroe.

soared. And where pop songwriters were obsessed by love, country tunesmiths preferred practical issues and real-life tragedies: mining, railroads, murders, and bank robberies were all grist to the mill.

KWKH Radio in Shreveport took the Louisiana Hayride to the

Above: Maybelle Carter, center, is flanked by Johnny Cash, right, and the Rev. Jimmy Snow on March 20, 1974, at the last Opry.

airwaves in 1948, but television was already waiting in the wings for pioneers like Gene Autry to exploit. He moved to the small screen with the introduction of the Gene Autry Show, to be swiftly followed by Roy Rogers. The Grand Ole Opry had enjoyed national broadcast status for some while and, from October 1955 to September 1956, ABC-TV aired an hour-long television version live from Nashville once a month on Saturday nights.

On October 2, 1954, a teenage Elvis Presley made his first and only radio performance at the Opry, and was introduced by Hank Snow. He performed a rocked-up version of Bill Monroe's "Blue Moon Of Kentucky," one side of his debut single. While the audience reacted politely, Opry manager Jim Denny reportedly advised him after the show to resume his truck-driving career. Presley swore never to return, and didn't.

Elvis, of course, would very soon change the face of American music with a black-influenced rock 'n' roll sound that made mainstream country seem somewhat tame by comparison. As the '50s continued, his Sun Records labelmates Jerry Lee Lewis, Carl Perkins, and Johnny Cash added elements of blues to country, and the music that emerged was known as "rockabilly." Its heyday was 1956, when the second, third, and fourth most popular songs on *Billboard*'s charts were Elvis Presley's "Heartbreak Hotel," Johnny Cash's "I Walk The Line," and Carl Perkins' "Blue Suede Shoes."

The rockabilly genre was, in Perkins' words, "blues with a country beat." As eminent writer Peter Guralnick elaborates, the hybrid was called rockabilly "because it wasn't the clankety rock of Bill Haley and his Comets, nor the hillbilly sound of Roy Acuff and Ernest Tubb, but a fusion of the two." Rockabilly survived as a pure genre through veterans like Charlie Feathers, plus a number of revival groups like the Stray Cats. The likes of Buddy Holly and the Everly Brothers also had strong country elements to their sound, particularly the bluegrass-inflected harmonies of Don and Phil that scored many pop hits. Their influence would, in turn, carry over into '60s pop: the Beatles and Hollies took their name, and something of their sound, from Buddy's band.

The sixties were a tougher time for country. These new groups' vibrant sounds cut into country record sales, radio airplay, and concert ticket sales. As Opry veteran Faron Young put it, the business reached a point where "a hillbilly couldn't get a job." Most of the artists profiled in this book had had their heyday and some would henceforth be seen as "heritage acts."

Country's response was a "Nashville Sound" purveyed by the likes of Jim Reeves, Ferlin Husky, Eddy Arnold, and George Jones. But in reality it was the studio producers, like Owen Bradley, Chet Atkins, Don Law, and, later, Billy Sherrill, that were now calling the shots. And their allies were a group of studio musicians known as the "A-Team" whose quick adaptability and creativity helped the hit-making process. It was a music machine that would create stars, but not as many would enjoy the longevity of the pioneers.

The Nashville Sound was notable for borrowing from '50s pop stylings: the basic recording was used as an instrumental "bed" onto which a string section and vocal chorus was overlaid to sweeten the sound. The lead vocal was smooth and upfront in the mix, while instrumental soloing was discouraged in favor of repeated phrases or "licks." So successful was the approach that in 1960, *Time* magazine reported that Nashville had "nosed out Hollywood as the nation's second biggest (after New York) record-producing center."

Country had first begun to sanitize its act in the early 1950s when *Billboard* magazine, at the suggestion of Ernest Tubb, replaced "hillbilly" as the heading atop their best-sellers chart with "country and western." Eventually, the industry would drop the "Western" part too, as it aimed for even wider acceptance. The National Academy of Recording Artists and Sciences changed their Grammy category to Country from Country & Western in 1968. Meanwhile, the pioneers were not to be forgotten: the Country Music Hall of Fame opened its doors in 1961 inducting Jimmie Rodgers, Fred Rose, and Hank Williams as its first members. Roy Acuff was soon to follow.

The country genre had thus far been almost exclusively male and white. But in the wake of Patsy Cline's late-'50s success, female singers were now entering the male-dominated genre and emerging as star performers. Cline and Kitty Wells led the way for Jean Shepard, Skeeter Davis, Dottie West, Connie Smith, Loretta Lynn, Barbara Mandrell, Tammy Wynette, and Dolly Parton to rise to the top.

As a music that had developed in the South, country had been as white as a snowdrift until, in 1962, blind singer-pianist Ray Charles vaulted the invisible color bar. Turning his attention from rhythm and blues to country, he scored hits with the album *Modern Sounds In Country And Western Music* and his cover of Don Gibson's "I Can't Stop Loving You." Two years later, Charley Pride became another black performer to be hailed as a country star.

In fact, the social change and political turmoil that characterized the 1960s was reflected in every facet of popular culture. And country music was no different. Some performers reaffirmed their faith in the genre's values and traditions, while others rebelled against the status quo. Nashville's proudly-worn reputation as Music City would soon face more than one challenge to its supremacy.

In the 1970s, Bakersfield, located one hundred miles northwest of Los Angeles, became a center for a hard-edged country music style. California's population had been swelled during the war with an influx of working-class Southerners who had moved out West to find work, a movement that had gone on since the Dust Bowl migration of the '30s. Now it was to nurture a new offshoot of country.

The Bakersfield sound mixed hardcore honky tonk with elements of Western swing, and was influenced by one-time residents Bob Wills and Lefty Frizzell. Merle Haggard, Ferlin Husky, and Buck Owens were leading progenitors of a style described by one critic as "sharp, hard, driving, no-frills and edgy." Dwight Yoakam is one of today's artists to have paid homage.

Next to challenge Nashville was Austin, Texas, the adopted home of Willie Nelson. The man who first came to prominence writing "Crazy" for Patsy Cline and "Hello Walls" for Faron Young headed for the Lone Star State after his Nashville house burned down, and liked it so much he decided to stay. His main contribution was to make country music fashionable to younger audience sated by rock's excesses.

Together with Eddie Wilson, a former PR for the state's beer industry, Nelson created a scene based around Armadillo World Headquarters, a former National Guard armory he converted and re-christened in 1972. The music evolved into a "progressive country" strain known as "the Austin sound" or "the Outlaw movement" as exemplified by his album *Wanted: The Outlaws*. He was joined on that recording by Waylon Jennings, Jessi Colter, and Tompall Glaser, while the likes of Kris Kristofferson, Johnny Cash, and Hank Williams, Jr. took advantage of Outlaw-inspired freedoms in their '70s output.

Nelson later insisted that, "The whole outlaw thing… had nothing to do with the music, it was something that got written in an article, and the young people said, 'Well, that's pretty cool.' And started listening."

Pop and country grew ever closer during the '70s, a merger that was not to everyone's liking. The Bellamy Brothers, Glen Campbell, John Denver, Anne Murray, and Olivia Newton-John all populated the country charts. And a furore ensued when the last-named performer, born in England and raised in Australia, won 1974's Best Female Country Vocal Performance and Female Vocalist of the Year awards. Worse was to come: when reigning Entertainer of the Year, Charlie Rich, presented the

award to his successor, John Denver, in 1975, he set fire to the envelope with a cigarette lighter as a protest against pop's "dilution" of the country music genre. Nevertheless, the dividing lines had been irrevocably blurred and, by the following decade, the likes of Kenny Rogers, Dolly Parton, Eddie Rabbitt, and Willie Nelson were straddling both charts with equal success.

The country-rock genre started when a number of rock bands made their way to Nashville and discover their "roots" in the wake of Bob Dylan's 1969 album *Nashville Skyline*. The Byrds were led there by Gram Parsons, a poor little rich boy who fancied his chances as a country singer: they cut one unsuccessful but ultimately influential album, *Sweetheart Of The Rodeo*, before he split to form the Flying Burrito Brothers and ultimately perish in the desert after a drugs overdose. Steel guitars and fiddles were prominent in his music, which latterly featured harmony vocals by the wonderful Emmylou Harris.

The seeds Parsons sowed would result in a smooth brand of West Coast country-rock as exemplified by the likes of Linda Ronstadt and, separately, her former backing band the Eagles. How much an album like 1976's mega-platinum *Hotel California* owes to country is debatable, but earlier efforts like "Desperado" featuring former Burrito Brother Bernie Leadon were worthy of the tag. More acts that would plough a country-rock furrow in the '80s included the Long Ryders and Tennessee's Jason and the Scorchers, while a related, but less commercial musical genre, Southern rock, was helmed by Lynyrd Skynyrd and the Allman Brothers.

The '80s was a largely forgettable decade for country as the "Urban Cowboy" movement held brief sway. The film of that name had popularized the country dance club scene then flourishing. However, the decade also saw the beginnings of New Country, or "countrypolitan," with the likes of Asleep at the Wheel, George Strait, and Reba McEntire incorporating elements of Western swing and bluegrass in their new music. The most successful country act of the decade in sales terms was Alabama, a band often credited with bringing country groups back into vogue. The band, led by Randy Owen, have over thirty Number 1 records on the *Billboard* country charts to their credit and have sold over seventy-three million records.

The '90s was the decade of the "hat act," a slightly pejorative term used to describe the likes of Garth Brooks. His *Ropin' the Wind* album debuted at Number 1 on the *Billboard* pop chart of 1991, inspiring a diverse array of performers to bring country to the younger generation. John Anderson, Randy Travis, Alan Jackson, Travis Tritt, and Clint Black were among the names to watch, while Lyle Lovett's eclectic musical mix even embraced big-band jazz.

Female vocalists were also on the rise in a new crop: Wynonna Judd and Patti Loveless were among the new queens of Nashville continuing to lean on tradition. Rosanne Cash and Mary Chapin Carpenter were feistier exponents of female country, setting the tone for Shania Twain to go multi-platinum. But there was still room for the glamorous country diva as exemplified by Faith Hill, Trisha Yearwood, and LeAnn Rimes.

Several male stars had matured and would peak in the '90s. Steve Earle was country's equivalent of Bruce Springsteen, bringing politics into his music, while Dwight Yoakam, who had debuted in 1984 in a simpler acoustic style, came of age in 1993 with "This Time." Another star in the making, Vince Gill, had fronted the Pure Prairie League before scoring solo hits with "Look At Us" and "I Still Believe In You," both in 1992.

These troubadours who, in previous decades, might have been grouped together

Above: Ryan Adams performs in Boston, 2005.

as singer-songwriters, had a very powerful new ally. Just as MTV had given pop a shot in the arm by broadcasting videos of top acts, so CMT (Country Music Television) aired country programming.

Alt.country became the "next big thing" in the late '90s. Uncle Tupelo, Wilco, and Whiskeytown—the latter led by future solo star Ryan Adams—all called on the legacy of Gram Parsons to add fizz to their band of country-rock. It was the most successful youth-aimed branch of country since Willie Nelson's Outlaw experiment. And when Adams and others of his ilk joined the likes of Bob Dylan and Emmylou Harris to record *Timeless*, a tribute album to Hank Williams just before the fiftieth anniversary of his passing, it re-emphasized that country's broad, all-inclusive church was still welcoming all comers.

Country today is in the rudest of health. While sales of most musical genres have declined, country experienced a boom year in 2006. The first six months of that year saw U.S. album sales of thirty-six million, an increase of nearly eighteen percent. Radio listening figures of around seventy-seven million adults have remained steady for almost a decade, while Garth Brooks, with over 128 million albums sold, has become the top-selling solo artist in U.S. history.

Country music, as Willie Nelson told us at the start of this introduction, is "a place where people tell their life stories." As life becomes increasingly complicated, so country has retained its appeal. The story has always come first, and one thing is certain— there are plenty more still to be told.

Ultimate crossover artist Parton wins Grammy Awards for Best Country Vocal Performance by a Female and Best Country Song and wins her first Academy of Country Music Female Vocalist of the Year award.

1982 The Bluebird Café opens in Nashville and becomes an important showcase for new talent hoping to be discovered.

1983 Country Music Television (CMT) beats TNN's

Nashville Network launch by two days, meaning that country music now had two cable television networks.

1984 Ralph Peer is inducted into the Country Music Hall of Fame.

Above: One of country's most innovative and legenday perfermoers, Willie Nelson.

1991 Garth Brooks creates sales records with his *Ropin' The Wind* album.

1993 Willie Nelson is inducted into the Country Music Hall of Fame.

1994 Johnny Cash's career resurgence begins when his *American Recordings* album is named Best Contemporary Folk Album at the Grammies.

1995 Shania Twain's *The Woman In Me* wins Best Country Album. It is her first Grammy win.

1998 Elvis Presley and Tammy Wynette are inducted into the Country Music Hall of Fame.

1999 Dolly Parton is inducted into the Country Music Hall of Fame.

2000 Charley Pride is inducted into the Country Music Hall of Fame.

Faith Hill earns three Grammys including Best Country Album for *Breathe*, Best Female Country Vocal Performance and Best Country Collaboration with Vocals for "Let's Make Love," her duet with husband Tim McGraw,

2001 Waylon Jennings is inducted into the Country Music Hall of Fame.

2003 June Carter Cash takes the Best Female Country Vocal performance Grammy for The Carter Family classic "Keep On The Sunny Side." *Her Wildwood Flower* is also named best traditional folk album. They are her final Grammys, as she dies in May.

2005 Garth Brooks signs up with Wal-Mart, giving the shop chain exclusivity on his product.

Above: Dolly Parton.

Below: Garth Brooks.

JIMMIE RODGERS

"This man really had guts. He was fired with a great ambition to be successful, both as an artist and financially. The impetus he gave to so-called hillbilly music set in motion the factors which resulted in making this sector of the amusement business into a matter of world-wide importance."
Ralph Peer, the man who signed him to RCA Victor

Country music can tell many stories of triumph over adversity, but that of Jimmie Rodgers is one of the more extreme. His mother died early of tuberculosis—the disease that would claim his own life in 1933—but even while he suffered from the disease Rodgers managed to work over a decade on the railroad, doing every job from water carrier to brakeman while strumming guitar or banjo during idle moments. The experience inspired many of his greatest songs and despite his health handicap Rodgers became a star of the Depression years, touring widely in the South and bringing music and cheer to people who sorely needed it.

James Charles Rodgers entered the world on September 8, 1897, in Meridian, Mississippi—the youngest of three boys born to Eliza Bozeman and Aaron Rodgers. His father was a section foreman on the railroad and work kept him from home much of the time. Eliza was a frail woman and died when Jimmie was four or five. Life was hard; Rodgers passed through several foster homes and had enjoyed little formal education when, aged fourteen, he followed his father into the rail yards at Meridian.

Young Jimmie started taking an interest in music after a spell living with his aunt Dora, a former music teacher. Songs were learned from his fellow rail workers, many black, who may also have given him lessons on the guitar and banjo. The simplicity, directness, and feeling in the blues they taught him became essential elements of his music. By now he had graduated from working as a water boy,

Left: Jimmie Rodgers, the "Singing Brakeman."

Right: A rare portrait of Rodgers as a young boy.

becoming a flagman and brakeman on the Meridian to New Orleans route.

Unfortunately, his health was already failing. Rodgers discharged himself from hospital in 1924 after a TB diagnosis (despite the fact the disease usually proved fatal) and nearly died from a pulmonary haemorrhage in 1925. By this time he had a wife, Carrie (his second, whom he married while she was still a schoolgirl), and daughter Anita to support: another daughter had died of diphtheria in 1923, aged six months, and on hearing that sad news, Rodgers had pawned his banjo to get the fare to return from New Orleans, where he'd been looking for work.

Knowing that he was suffering from the same illness that had killed his mother, Rodgers moved to Asheville, North Carolina, where the mountain air was more conducive to good health. Here, he tried his hand at earning a living as an entertainer, even working in a tent show. In February 1927, Asheville's first radio station, WWNC, went on the air and in April broadcast Rodgers performing for the first time. A few months later, he recruited a group from Tennessee called the Tenneva Ramblers—Jack and Claude Grant and Jack Pierce—though they soon walked out on him after a row about billing.

From this low ebb, Rodgers' fortunes were to turn around dramatically. When Victor talent scout Ralph Peer recorded him in a third floor Bristol, Tennessee, hotel room in 1927, history was made. Rodgers and The Carter Family were discovered on the same day and both would become hugely influential after Peer recorded them. The two songs he cut that day were "The Soldier's Sweetheart" and "Sleep, Baby, Sleep." Rodgers was a very distinctive guitarist, and Ralph Peer would later recall: "He was an individualist [with] his own way of selecting his chords, and was what can best be described as a 'natural' guitar player. I remember that another artist, during the year of 1931, spent a great deal of time learning one of Jimmie's 'wrong' chords. Whatever he used always sounded right, but upon examination it was quite often not the chord which would ordinarily have been used."

The two songs recorded that day were well enough received for Rodgers to travel to the Victor headquarters in Camden, New Jersey, in late November to record four

Above, left to right: A still from the "Singing Brakeman" film; with musician Clayton McMichen; Rodgers with the Tenneva Ramblers.

"He sang the songs of the people he loved, of a young nation growing strong. His was an America of glistening rails, thundering boxcars, and rain-swept night, of lonesome prairies, great mountains, and a high blue sky. He sang of the bayous and the cornfields, the wheated plains, of the little towns, the cities, and of the winding rivers of America."

Inscription on Jimmie Rodgers' statue in Meridian, Mississippi

more. From this second session came the immortal "Blue Yodel #1," better known as "T For Texas," Rodgers' first big hit.

Three more songs made it out of this session: "Ben Dewberry's Final Run," "Mother Was A Lady," and "Away Out On The Mountain." Over the next two years, the disc that paired "T for Texas" with "Away Out On The Mountain" sold nearly half a million copies. Rodgers was acclaimed as a star, and having worked on the railroad soon became known as the "Singing Brakeman."

Within months he was on his way to national stardom—playing theaters, broadcasting regularly from Washington, D.C., and signing for a vaudeville tour of major Southern cities. (He never toured north of the Mason Dixon line.) With his earnings he built a large home in Kerrville, Texas, though this later had to be sold after medical expenses took their toll and the Depression reduced audiences. For the time being though times were good. Royalties and income from recordings improved his quality of life, and he was generous to a fault with his new wealth. When he received a cheque, Jimmie would share it with friends and relatives, though one of those relatives paid her own way. Jimmie's piano-playing sister-in-law, Elsie McWilliams, had been in a three-piece dance band with Jimmie and fiddler Slim Rozell in the early days, and she now composed and collaborated with him during the early part of his recording career.

Rodgers went on to star in a short film, *The Singing Brakeman*, tour with humorist Will Rogers, and record with The Carter Family, Clayton McMichen, and Bill Boyd. He was one of the first white stars to work with black musicians, recording with St. Louis bluesman Clifford Gibson, while in July 1930 he recorded "Blue Yodel #9" (also known as "Standin' On The Corner") with Louis Armstrong (whose wife, Lillian, played piano).

THE CARTER FAMILY

"Growing up I took all this stuff for granted. I was into rock and heavy metal. There's an innocence, great charm, and raw beauty that came through their music." John Carter Cash, June's grandson

The Carter Family were the first group to make a name for themselves in country, and command an unique place in music history. Along with A.P. Carter the other founding members were A.P.'s wife Sara (born Sara Dougherty in 1898) and sister-in-law Maybelle. Sara sang lead and played autoharp, while Maybelle added harmony as well as playing the melody on the bass strings of her guitar, a picking style that became known as the "Carter scratch." Maybelle's ability to also keep the rhythm going on the higher strings would prove influential on later flatpickers such as Doc Watson, Clarence White, and Norman Blake. Before The Carter Family's recordings, the guitar was rarely used as a lead or solo instrument by white musicians, but the combination of a melodic line on the bass strings with intermittent strumming is now a staple of the steel string guitarist's repertoire.

Alvin Pleasant "A.P." Carter was born in 1891 in Poor Valley (known now as Maces Springs), Virginia, the first of eight children of Robert and Mollie Bays Carter. Nearly struck by lightning during her pregnancy, Mollie later ascribed the quaver for which her son's singing would become known to that near miss. While working in 1914,

Left: The Carter Family (from left to right) Maybelle Carter, Alvin P. Carter, and Sara Carter.

selling trees and shrubs for his uncle's nursery, A.P. Carter walked over the mountain to Rich Valley to make a sale to his Aunt Susie. As he approached the house, he heard Sara Dougherty singing. They fell in love and married the following year.

A.P. and Sara auditioned for a Brunswick Record talent scout in Kingsport, Tennessee, in 1926 but, since Sara was then the lead singer, he passed, telling them a musical group with a female lead singer would never sell records. There was better luck to be had the following year when A.P. saw an announcement in the local newspaper for auditions being held by the Victor record label in Bristol, Tennessee. On July 31, 1927, A.P. drove his Model A Ford the twenty-five miles from Maces Spring, Virginia, to Bristol, Tennessee, to record for talent scout Ralph Peer. The rewards offered by Victor were great in that immediate pre-Depression period—a generous $50 per song. The Carter Family were successful and later the same year Victor released a double-sided 78rpm record of the group performing "Wandering Boy" and "Poor Orphan Child." In 1928, "The Storms Are On The Ocean" and "Single Girl, Married Girl" were paired on another record, which also became very popular.

In May, 1928, Ralph Peer called the Carters to Victor's base in Camden, New Jersey, for additional recording sessions and the following February they returned for a third time. As previously, Peer paid them $50 per song, plus royalties on copyrightable songs. They would carry on this association until 1933, to the benefit of both parties. Indeed, by their career's end they'd recorded around 300 old-time ballads, traditional tunes, country songs, and gospel hymns; all representative of America's Southern folklore and heritage.

In fact, A.P. was a master at reworking traditional songs by giving them memorable melodies. Unlike their new-found labelmate Jimmie Rodgers, who'd shown up at Bristol the same day as themselves, The Carter Family showed few jazz or blues influences, their hymn-like harmonies representing a pure white Appalachian sound.

With the prospect of profiting from each new song he collected and copyrighted, A.P. traveled around the southwestern Virginia area with Lesley "Esley" Riddle, a black guitar player from Kingsport, Tennessee. And while A.P. was out on the road collecting songs, Sara fell in love with his cousin, Coy Bays, and subsequently had an affair with him. Coy's parents moved to California, taking their

"I read a quote one time, it summed up my take on The Carter Family. It said, 'In the presence of perfect beauty, tears are the only answer.' The Carter Family is about as pure and close to the source as you can get." Singer Marty Stuart

son with them to defuse the situation and Sara returned to her childhood home in Rich Valley, leaving the children with A.P. After three years of trying to reconcile with her husband, she sued for divorce, even while the family continued to perform together professionally.

The Carter Family reached a new audience in the late 1930s via border radio station XERA which, broadcasting from Mexico, was unregulated by authorities in the States and had a far more powerful, wide-ranging signal than its competitors. Johnny Cash in Arkansas, Waylon Jennings in Texas, Chet Atkins in Georgia, and Tom T. Hall in Kentucky all listened and learned from The Carter Family.

The Family operated out of their homes in the Clinch Mountain area of Virginia until 1938, when they moved to Texas for three years, and then to Charlotte, North Carolina. By now Sara had divorced A.P. and married Coy Bayes, with whom she had been reunited after dedicating a song to him on XERA in early 1939. Coy, living in California with his parents, heard the song, went to Texas

Right: (From left to right) June, Anita, Helen with Maybelle (seated).

Above: Johnny Cash, his wife June Carter and their son John.

Left: Janette Carter, the last surviving child of A.P. and Sara, during a tribute to the Carter Family at the Smithsonian Folklife Festival in 2003.

to find her, and the pair married on February 20, in Brackettsville, near Del Rio.

In 1941, Mexico and the United States signed a broadcasting treaty that effectively shut down XERA. The Carter family broadcast for two more years on a local radio station in Charlotte, North Carolina, before disbanding, though the doughty Maybelle recruited daughters Helen, Anita, and June to keep the tradition going. (A.P., Maybelle, and Maybelle's daughters met for a musical reunion in Knoxville in 1948, giving a number of performances on WNOX radio.) The girls also performed on their own as the more modern-sounding Carter Sisters, but it was June Carter who would enjoy the greatest public profile. She joined Johnny Cash's touring group in 1962, eventually persuading him to take on her mother and sisters as well. Johnny and June fell in love, and after a long courtship the pair finally wed on June 1, 1968. But June remained a Carter, saying: "How can you be any purer than pure if your name is Carter? How can you get away from being a Carter? There's a part of you that's gonna come through. How do you keep from doing it? It's what you're born to do."

Grandes dames Maybelle and Sara enjoyed one last hurrah at the 1967 Newport Folk Festival. Little was thereafter heard of Sara, but she came out of retirement at her daughter Janette's request in 1975 to play a show with Maybelle at the Carter Fold in Maces Springs. Maybelle died in 1978, Sara the year after.

In 1970, exactly a decade after A.P.'s passing, the Family was honored by the Country Music Hall of Fame, the first group to win the accolade. The citation read: "They are regarded by many as the epitome of country greatness and originators of a much copied style." Proof of this could be seen as early as the 1960s when folk singers like Joan Baez, Pete Seeger, and Odetta had performed many of the songs the Carters had collected or written. "The Wayworn Traveller" was covered by a young Bob Dylan whose first attempt to add his own words to the melody resulted in "Paths Of Victory," while a change of time signature and lyrics resulted in one of his most famous songs, "The Times They Are A-Changin'." Dylan was following the lead of his hero, Woody Guthrie, who had similarly used "When This World's On Fire" as the inspiration for "This Land Is Your Land."

The Carter Family's legacy and influence continues unabated. Today's alt.country giants Uncle Tupelo named their 1990 album *No Depression* after one of their songs and two years later, the U.S. Postal Service issued a commemorative postage stamp honoring A.P., Sara, and Maybelle. In 2001, the group was inducted into the International Bluegrass Music Hall of Honor, receiving a Grammy Lifetime Achievement Award four years later. Although the last survivor—June Carter Cash—died in 2003, the music of "The First Family of Country Music" lives on.

THE CARTER FAMILY

FORMED: 1926?

DISBANDED: 1943

INSTRUMENTS: Singers, guitar

FIRST RECORDED: 1927

INFLUENCES: Gospel music

RECOMMENDED LISTENING

Volume 1: 1927-1928—Anchored In Love (1993)

Volume 2: 1928-1929—My Clinch Mountain Home (1993)

Clinch Mountain Treasures (1991)

Country Music Hall Of Fame Series (1991)

ROY ACUFF

"The greatest thing the Democrats have ever done for me was to defeat me for the governor of Tennessee." Roy Acuff

The clash between the sacred and the secular has been one of the longest-running themes through popular music—and American popular music in particular. Country has traditionally kept a foot in both camps by paying lip service to gospel music, both in style and content. Wind the clock back to the early '30s, though, and one can only wonder what Roy Acuff's father, a devout Baptist minister, felt when his son decided to forge a career in secular music. In the event, the Rev. Neill Acuff had little to worry about: his son's training in church proved a big influence on his work. And when war broke out, in the words of country music historian Bill C. Malone, the comforting sounds Roy purveyed "seemed to suggest all the verities for which Americans were fighting: home, mother, and God."

Despite his God-fearing image, Roy Claxton Acuff, born on September 15, 1903, in Maynardsville, Tennessee, started life as something of a wild child. His dream was to be a professional sportsman. A star athlete in high school, he played semiprofessional baseball and basketball after graduation and eventually tried out for the New York Yankees. Unfortunately, a series of sunstrokes confined him to bed for the better part of 1929 and 1930, forcing him to give up his dreams of a sporting career.

Left: The great Roy Acuff on stage.

The next stop was showbusiness. He learned to play the fiddle (father Neill had been an amateur fiddle player) and early musical influences included Fiddlin' John Carson and Gid Tanner and the Skillet Lickers. He joined a local medicine show, where he learned how to capture and entertain an audience, and after a year moved on to form his own group, The Tennessee Crackerjacks, who broadcast on a local radio station. Their signature instrument was the Dobro (or resonator guitar), played by Clell Summey, and the distinctive whining sound, not unlike a Hawaiian guitar, came to be associated with Acuff.

yelling, "To hell with Roosevelt, to hell with Babe Ruth, to hell with Roy Acuff."

Aside from his music, the other major legacy Roy Acuff left was the first publishing house dedicated to country music—Acuff-Rose Music, founded in 1942 with Fred Rose. Their joint names still appear as copyright holders to many legendary songs. Acuff first discovered that there was a potential goldmine in music publishing when he printed his own songbook and sold a staggering 100,000 copies. Although publishers in New York tried to acquire the rights to his songs, the success of the songbook convinced Acuff to seek out the help of Rose, a professional songwriter and pianist working in Chicago.

Above: Richard Nixon and Roy Acuff at the Grand Ole Opry.

"A little secret of my policy in the studio... Whenever you once decide that you are going to record a number, put everything you've got into it. Don't say, 'Oh, we'll take it over and do it again,' because every time you go through it you lose just a little something. Let's do it the first time and to hell with the rest of them." Roy Acuff

Acuff-Rose Publications started with Acuff's songs as its base, but Rose also added his songs, including "Faded Love," "Deep Water," and "Blue Eyes Crying In The Rain." Eventually, the company would come to own huge numbers of copyrights including songs by Marty Robbins, Felice and Boudleaux Bryant, and all the songs of Hank Williams.

Around this time Acuff had a brief career in politics, campaigning unsuccessfully as a Republican to become the governor of Tennessee in 1944 and 1948. But he remained a power in the country music business; the character played by Henry Gibson in Robert Altman's film *Nashville*, Haven Hamilton, was said to have been modeled in part on Acuff's career. He was also one of the first country musicians to appear on television.

Roy Acuff recorded for a number of labels including Hickory Records, which he and Fred Rose owned, but his sales declined in the late 1940s and '50s and he spent most of his time on the road around this time. He didn't have a single chart record between 1947 and 1958, returning with the Top 10 hit "Once More," as well as two other Top 20 singles, "So Many Times" and "Come And Knock."

By 1962, when Acuff became the first living member of the Country Music Hall of Fame, he had sold more than 25 million records. Three years later he suffered severe injuries in an auto accident and cut back his touring schedule to spend more time working on a country music museum. This is now at Opryland U.S.A., where the Opry moved from downtown Nashville in 1974. Acuff was the host of the opening ceremonies.

Roy Acuff joined the Nitty Gritty Dirt Band for its 1972 tribute to mountain music, *Will the Circle Be Unbroken*, and the following year became the oldest performer to have a record on the charts with "Back In The Country." As his health began to decline in the late 1980s, he built a house near the Opry so he could greet friends and fans. This was a difficult period for Acuff, as he experienced the death of his wife and several longtime band members, including pianist Jimmie Riddle and fiddler Howdy Forrester. In 1987, he released his final charting record, a version of "The Precious Jewel" recorded with Charlie Louvin of the Louvin Brothers.

Acuff the singer was a major influence on the likes of George Jones, who heard him on Grand Old Opry; Jones' high notes still betray an influence in the phrasing. Hank Williams also once said: "I was a pretty good imitator of Roy Acuff, but then I found out they already had a Roy Acuff, so I started singin' like myself."

In December 1991, Acuff was honored during a televised ceremony at the Kennedy Center in Washington for his contribution to the performing arts. Among his other honors were the National Medal of Art in July (received in 1991) and in 1987 he was given a Lifetime Achievement Award by the National Academy of Recording Arts and Sciences, the organization that presents the Grammy awards.

Known as the King of Country Music, Roy Acuff lived up to that title for more than sixty years. At the time of his death in November 1992, he was still actively involved in the Grand Ole Opry, and was as popular as ever.

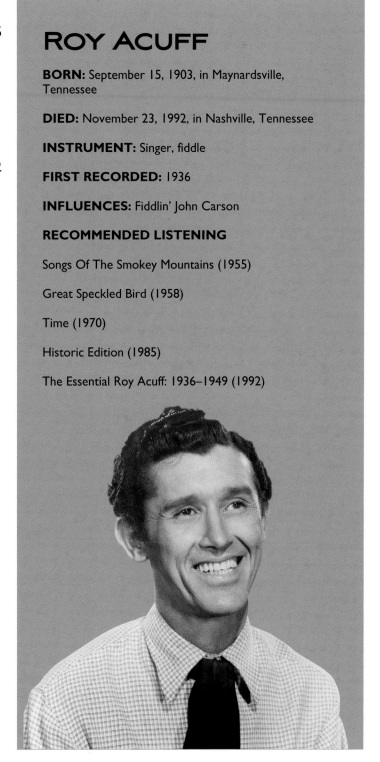

ROY ACUFF

BORN: September 15, 1903, in Maynardsville, Tennessee

DIED: November 23, 1992, in Nashville, Tennessee

INSTRUMENT: Singer, fiddle

FIRST RECORDED: 1936

INFLUENCES: Fiddlin' John Carson

RECOMMENDED LISTENING

Songs Of The Smokey Mountains (1955)

Great Speckled Bird (1958)

Time (1970)

Historic Edition (1985)

The Essential Roy Acuff: 1936–1949 (1992)

BOB WILLS & HIS TEXAS PLAYBOYS

"Rock and Roll? Why, man, that's the same kind of music we've been playin' since 1928! We didn't call it rock and roll back when we introduced it as our style, and we don't call it rock and roll the way we play it now. But it's just basic rhythm and has gone by a lot of different names in my time."
Bob Wills

Developed in Texas and Oklahoma in the 1930s, Western swing blended various disparate musical elements, notably big band, blues, Dixieland, and jazz, to create great dance music. Bob Wills, the "King of Western Swing," was the man behind it all, and his contribution was officially recognized, albeit decades later, when he was elected to the Country Music Hall of Fame in 1968.

James Robert Wills was brought up on the Kosse, Texas, ranch where he was born on March 6, 1905. It was said that all his relations were "farmers, barbers, or musicians," and, indeed, his father was a statewide champion fiddle player who taught him all the traditional fiddle tunes of the Southwest. The Wills family frequently held country dances in their home with a sister and brother playing guitar, while another sister played piano.

The fiddle came into Wills' life when he was ten, and a few short years later he was entertaining listeners of local radio stations. He had spent much of his younger life playing with black children, and learned some traditional Negro songs from them. "I don't know whether they made them up as they moved down the cotton rows or not," Wills once told Charles Townsend, author of *San Antonio Rose: The Life And Times Of Bob Wills*, "but they sang blues you never heard before." Added to this was the influence of jazz, which he heard via the relatively new-fangled means of radio. Even Mexican music from across the nearby border was grist to his mill. It all came together in a fascinatingly diverse range of musical sounds and styles upon which the young Wills could and would draw again and again.

He ended the 1920s in Forth Worth, Texas, where he had become a barber by profession and a musician at night. By this time Wills' had come together with a

Left: Bob Wills (at the front with the fiddle) with Gene Autry from 1937.

THE LIGHT CRUST DOUGHBOYS

"The Doughboys embodied the very essence of the 'golden era' of radio-live performances and the dominance of programming by advertising agencies." Doughboys archivist John Mark Dempsey

Despite their somewhat unlikely name, The Light Crust Doughboys at one time included in their line-up both a Governor of Texas and the most influential Western swing musician of all time. While their name may not be familiar to many younger country music fans, the Western swing-styled band, which was launched over three quarters of a century ago, achieved and retained fame as the first notable band in which the legendary "King Of Western Swing," Bob Wills, was a member. They first performed in 1931, but, incredibly, are still the finest, most successful, and certainly the longest-lived Western swing band in the Dallas/Fort Worth area of Texas today.

In 1929, Bob Wills moved from West Texas to Fort Worth, where he formed the Wills Fiddle Band, a somewhat impressive title for what was, in fact, only a duo. The other member was Herman Arnspiger, on guitar. During the following year, the duo became a trio with the addition of vocalist Milton Brown, and in 1931 the Wills Fiddle Band, still a trio, became The Light Crust Doughboys after Wills convinced Burrus Mill and Elevator Company to sponsor the band on a radio show by advertising the mill's Light Crust Flour. Nevertheless, after only two weeks of broadcasts, Wilbert Lee "Pappy" O'Daniel, president of

Left: The Light Crust Doughboys at the Grammy Awards, 2006.

Burrus Mill, canceled the show because he found their "hillbilly music" not to his taste. At this time Milton Brown's brother, Durwood, joined the band as second guitarist, and banjoist Clifford "Sleepy" Johnson arrived not long after. The group landed a regular radio gig in Fort Worth sponsored by the Aladdin Lamp Company and accordingly changed their name once again. This time to the Aladdin Laddies.

However, inspired by Wills' persistence and the demands of thousands of fans, a compromise was agreed whereby the group returned to the airwaves under the name The Light Crust Doughboys as long as the three musicians worked in the mill as well as performing. Fans would listen every day at midday for Wills playing the fiddle and Truett Kimsey's extraordinarily enthusiastic introduction: "The Light Crust Doughboys are on the air!" The trio would then start the show with their theme song, which became so popular that it remained their calling card long after: "Listen everybody, from near and far. If you want to know who we are. We're the Light Crust Doughboys from Burrus Mill."

O'Daniel realized that he was on to a good thing and decided to become the show's compere. He also arranged that it should be broadcast on several more radio stations throughout Texas as well as in much of Oklahoma. Soon it had become one of the most popular shows in the region attracting big audiences. However, the band members began leaving in 1932 when Milton Brown formed his own band, the Musical Brownies. The following year saw the departure of Wills, who was fired by O'Daniel for unreliability—largely due to excessive drinking.

Later in 1933, O'Daniel recruited a new band to be the Doughboys, and they went to a studio in Chicago to record for Vocalion Records. O'Daniel continued as manager and announcer until 1935, when he and Burrus Mill fell out, at which point he formed his own company, Hillbilly Flour, and a new band, the Hillbilly Boys, who he used in his successful bid as a Democrat for the governorship of Texas in 1938.

Meanwhile, back at Burrus Mill, between 1935 and 1940 The Light Crust Doughboys enjoyed their greatest success as many of the best Western swing musicians joined the band. Included in the line-up were fiddlers Clifford Gross and Kenneth Pitts, along with guitarist Dick

Reinhart; Marvin "Smokey" Montgomery on tenor banjo; Ramon DeArman on bass; and pianist John "Knocky" Parker, plus lead guitarist Muryel "Zeke" Campbell and another fiddler, Cecil Brower.

During the Second World War, the band dispersed as members served Uncle Sam and by 1942 the radio show was off the air. Although Burrus Mill relaunched the band at the end of the war, the magic seemed to have disappeared. By then radio had been almost forgotten as audiences turned on their new televisions.

This might have spelled the end for the Light Crust Doughboys, who were no longer "on the air," but— perhaps surprisingly—it didn't. The key to revival in the group's fortunes came in 1973, when band members were involved in sessions in Dallas for what turned out to be the final Bob Wills recordings, released as the album *For The Last Time*. For the rest of the 1970s and much of the '80s, tenor banjo player Marvin "Smokey" Montgomery, who had assumed control of the band, kept it alive in one form or another. When he died in 2001, an obituary claimed that he had been a Doughboy for an amazing sixty-five years. When the Texas Western Swing Hall of Fame was established in the late 1980s, The Light Crust Doughboys were the first act to be inducted.

The band had found their second wind. Multi-instrumentalist and successful songwriter—songs he has written have been recorded by Trini Lopez, Jewel Akens, and Engelbert Humperdinck, among others—Art Greenhaw, who was co-producing the band's records, decided to introduce a horn section. Dubbed "country

Fort Worth ...the way we were.

Burrus Mills...and its Light Crust Doughboys

From the Jack White Collection of Historic Fort Worth Photos, University of Texas at Arlington.

1949 view of Burrus Mills in far north Fort Worth. Burrus executive W. Lee O'Daniel used radio broadcasts and public appearances of the Light Crust Doughboys as a power base to become Texas governor and later senator. Please pass the biscuits!

THE LIGHT CRUST DOUGHBOYS

RECOMMENDED LISTENING

Doughboy Rock (2000)

We Called Him Mr. Gospel Music: The James Blackwood Tribute Album (2003)

Southern Meets Soul: An American Gospel Jubilee (2005)

Light Crust Doughboys 1936-1941 (2007)

Favourite Guitar and Banjo Classics Vol I. (2002)

jazz," the sound was heavily influenced by the original Western swing sound. In 1995, the Doughboys received the great honor of becoming "official music ambassadors of the Lone Star State."

Surprisingly, one of the band's 1930s recordings, "Pussycat, Pussycat, Pussycat," written by Montgomery, was featured in the 1996 movie *Striptease*, which starred Demi Moore and Burt Reynolds. Perhaps as an antidote to recognition in such an erotic film, by the end of the Twentieth Century, The Doughboys were also recording gospel music with James Blackwood of the Blackwood Brothers Quartet. In the late 1990s, The Light Crust Doughboys provided a live soundtrack to the Lone Star Ballet in Amarillo and performed with the Abilene Philharmonic, the Fort Worth Symphony, and the Dallas Wind Symphony. They were inducted into the Rockabilly Hall of Fame in 2000 and, sadly, played at Montgomery's funeral in 2001, after which Art Greenhaw assumed control of the group. In 2005, the Light Crust Doughboys Hall of Fame and Museum opened in Quitman, Texas, with a display of memorabilia relating to the group and live shows. A book detailing the history of the group was published in 2002. In 2003, the band won a Grammy for their part in a tribute album to James Blackwood and were nominated for another Grammy in 2005 for *Southern Meets Soul: An American Gospel Jubilee.*

"They were part of the tradition of rockabilly. The Doughboys' innovative Texas swing has a direct link to rock 'n' roll." Bob Timmers, founder of the Rockabilly Hall of Fame

GENE AUTRY

"Gene Autry is one of the most famous men, not only in America, but in the world." On his induction into the Cowboy Hall of Fame of Great Westerners

The genre of the singing cowboy, which was massively popular in the movies and television from the mid-1930s until the early '60s, was virtually invented by Gene Autry, who remains one of its greatest stars. Whether or not he was the most successful of the Western troubadours may be open to question, but many sources feel that Gene Autry was the first and best of the Hollywood singing cowboys.

Gene Autry was born Orvon Autry on September 29, 1907, in Tioga Springs, Texas, the son of Delbert Autry, a peripatetic tenant farmer. His father was always on the look out for work that would improveme his family's lifestyle, which resulted in his son (the oldest of four siblings) growing up in both Texas and Oklahoma. Gene's grandfather was a Baptist preacher who encouraged him to sing in order that the boy could join the church choir, while his father similarly taught him equestrian skills so that he could do farm work. As a youngster Gene showed musical promise. The first instrument he played was the saxophone, but he changed to the guitar at the age of twelve, as it enabled him to sing the cowboy songs he enjoyed.

After leaving school in 1924, Autry went to work as a railway telegrapher in Oklahoma and one night played and sang for a passing stranger who turned out to be the entertainer Will Rogers. Rogers recommended that Autry

practice his art by working in radio; advice which was heeded. By 1929, Autry had become known as "Oklahoma's Yodelling Cowboy" and had his own show at station KVOO in Tulsa, Oklahoma. His yodeling can be seen as the young star following the style of Jimmie Rodgers, though Autry abandoned it later in his career.

849 - Home of Gene Autry, North Hollywood, California

Left and right: Gene Autry (left) and his California home (right).

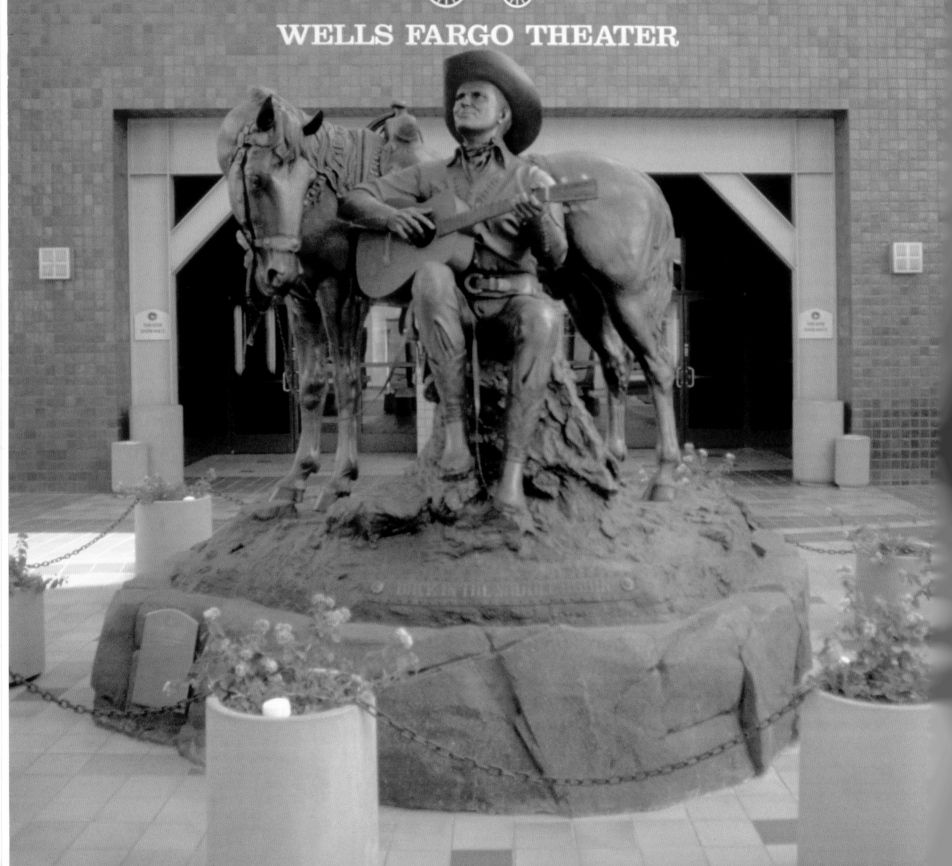

"Autry's film career skyrocketed, though his recording career developed at a slower pace. Despite a few classics like 'Riding Down The Canyon'... there was a stilted, old fashioned quality to much of his '30s output."

The Definitive Illustrated Encyclopedia Of Country Music

& Sciences, and the Board of Directors Lifetime Achievement Award from the International Achievement in Arts Foundation. Gene Autry was also inducted into the Nashville Songwriters Hall of Fame, The National Cowboy Hall of Fame, the National Association of Broadcasters Hall of Fame, and he received the Songwriters Guild Life Achievement Award. He was also honored by his songwriting peers with a lifetime achievement award from ASCAP. A measure of his integrity is that during the late 1930s, Autry turned down an offer of $3,000 (a small fortune in those days) to endorse a brand of cigarette.

Gene Autry died at his home in Studio City, California, on October 2, 1998. He was ninety-one years old. He remains a legend, and every bit of the praise that has been heaped upon him is extremely well-deserved.

Left: A bronze sculpture of Gene Autry and Champion outside the Autry Museum of Western Heritage.

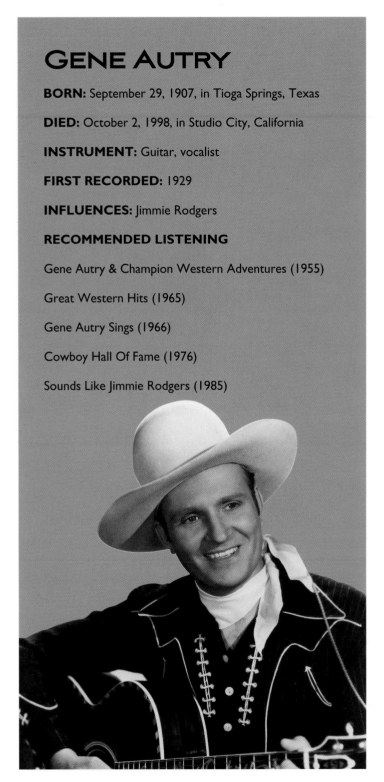

GENE AUTRY

BORN: September 29, 1907, in Tioga Springs, Texas

DIED: October 2, 1998, in Studio City, California

INSTRUMENT: Guitar, vocalist

FIRST RECORDED: 1929

INFLUENCES: Jimmie Rodgers

RECOMMENDED LISTENING

Gene Autry & Champion Western Adventures (1955)

Great Western Hits (1965)

Gene Autry Sings (1966)

Cowboy Hall Of Fame (1976)

Sounds Like Jimmie Rodgers (1985)

Bill Monroe

"As a musician, showman, composer, and teacher, Mr. Monroe has been a cultural figure and force of signal importance in our time... [We recognize] his many contributions to American culture and his many ways of helping American people enjoy themselves." U.S. Senate resolution, 1986

Monroe is often referred to as "the Father of Bluegrass" and his great contribution to music in general and country music in particular is undeniable. Nevertheless, popular recognition of his individual style was a long time coming. Country was first highlighted as a genre by Billboard magazine in the early 1950s, when "Country and Western" replaced "folk" and even "hillbilly" at the top of the bestsellers chart, but bluegrass remained off the media radar. Indeed, according to Ralph Stanley, it existed for a long time under another name: "Back then... it was just called old time mountain hillbilly music. When they started doing the bluegrass festivals in 1965, everybody got together and wanted to know what to call the show. It was decided that since Bill [Monroe] was the oldest man, and was from the Bluegrass state of Kentucky and he had the Blue Grass Boys, it would be called bluegrass."

Born William Smith Monroe in Rosine, Kentucky, on September 13, 1911, Monroe's performing career spanned sixty years as a singer, instrumentalist, composer, and bandleader. He was the youngest of eight children on the family farm and with an eight-year age gap to his nearest brother as well as poor eyesight, Monroe took refuge in music from an early age. Encouraged by his mother, Malissa, Bill and his siblings played and sang, with brothers Birch and Charlie on the fiddle and guitar, leaving Bill with the mandolin. Even then, his brothers insisted he remove four of

Left: Bill Monroe, the "Father of Bluegrass Music," in Nashville, 1984.

the eight strings from the instrument so that he would not play too loudly. In fact, both Malissa and her brother, Pendleton "Pen" Vandiver, were keen musicians and when his mother died, ten-year-old Bill went to live with his uncle. His musical education continued apace and he often accompanied Pendleton when he played the fiddle at local dances. This experience later inspired one of Monroe's most famous compositions, "Uncle Pen," recorded in 1950.

The three brothers (Birch on fiddle, Charlie on guitar, and Bill on mandolin) were offered full-time employment in 1934 by Radio WLS in Chicago. Birch soon retired from full-time music, but Charlie and Bill remained and became the Monroe Brothers. Now a duo, they hit their stride after moving in 1935 to the Carolinas, where they based themselves at Charlotte and North Carolina's 50,000-watt WBT. Here, their driving tempos, distinctive harmony, and Bill's lightning-fast mandolin solos soon won them a following.

In 1936, RCA producer Eli Oberstein recorded them for the first time. Early releases like the traditional hymn "What Would You Give in Exchange For Your Soul" sold well, and the duo earned a sizable regional audience with help from WBT's strong signal. However, the Monroes fell out, as brothers do, and broke up in 1938.

Undeterred, Bill formed the Kentuckians and moved to Radio KARK in Atlanta, Georgia, where the first of the Blue Grass Boys line-ups took shape. At this time, he also began to sing lead and take mandolin solos rather than merely contributing to the general sound. In 1939, Monroe auditioned for the Grand Ole Opry and George Hay was impressed enough by the performance of his trademark "Mule Skinner Blues," (formerly a hit for the legendary Jimmie Rodgers), to sign him. As Monroe would later recall, "I went in to audition and Harry Stone, Manager of the

"I'm a farmer with a mandolin and a high tenor voice." Bill Monroe

Opry and George D. Hay, The Solemn Old Judge, were going out to lunch, but they told me they would be right back. When they came back, we played some tunes for them, and they hired me right there. They told me, 'If you ever leave the Opry, you'll have to fire yourself.'" In fact, Monroe would be a member of the Grand Ole Opry for almost fifty-eight years.

The basic mandolin-guitar-fiddle-bass line-up he would always retain was now augmented by the banjo-first played by "Stringbean" (Dave Akeman), and then Earl Scruggs—while Monroe also experimented briefly with the accordion (which his mother had played in his youth) and harmonica. It proved a successful formula: by 1943 Monroe was grossing some $200,000 a year from live shows. Scruggs' distinctive driving banjo style had been added to Monroe's bluegrass sound in 1945. He remained with Bill until 1948, and along with guitarist/harmony vocalist Lester Flatt, whose laconic lead vocals were the perfect foil to Monroe's high tenor voice, was one of many famous musicians to pass through the ranks. (Flatt and Scruggs were later to team up again as the Foggy Mountain Boys.) "Bluegrass Breakdown" remains a test piece for aspiring bluegrass banjo players today.

Right: Monroe plays his mandolin in 1958.

74

Above: Monroe performs on stage, aged eighty.

Monroe stoically accepted that his band members would eventually fly the nest, at one time saying, "You know, they only stay with the Blue Grass Boys for about three years, and they get to be heard on the Opry, and I call their name when they play or sing, and that's good for them. They get to be known, and they can use that when they go on to their own bands."

When "Blue Moon Of Kentucky" was recorded by Elvis Presley, bluegrass music made the mainstream for the first time. Backing an Arthur Crudup blues number, "That's All Right," it was released as Sun 209 less than a fortnight later and introduced the world to rock 'n' roll. Presley, of course, hit the Hollywood highway and bluegrass retreated to its former cult status. But rumor has it that, when the King met

Bill and apologized for his handiwork, Monroe confided that he now played the hit version himself!

Banjo would never be featured as prominently in Monroe's music after Earl Scruggs left, testament to his talents. Instead, he hired guitarist/vocalist Jimmie Martin, plus fiddlers Vassar Clements and Buddy Spicher, experimenting with a twin-fiddle sound incorporating a drone to evoke his Appalachian heritage. The early 1960s also saw him join forces with mandolinist Ralph Rinzler, who helped connect him with the folk revival by persuading the Decca label to release Monroe's hard-to-find 1950s recordings on LP. He also acted as Monroe's agent, booking him at folk festivals, while the year of 1965 saw Monroe headlining the first multi-day bluegrass festival.

"If you want to know where my music comes from, listen to my record out called 'My Last Day On Earth.' That says it for me." Bill Monroe

In 1967, Bill Monroe launched his own annual festival at Bean Blossom, Indiana, where he ran a country music park. By 1970, when he won election to the Country Music Hall of Fame, he had become the acknowledged patriarch of the bluegrass movement and a cult figure to hordes of fans for whom bluegrass was akin to a religion. As Monroe himself said, "Bluegrass has brought more people together and made more friends than any music in the world. You meet people at festivals and renew acquaintances year after year."

By this time, Monroe's band had again become a school for aspiring bluegrass musicians. The likes of Peter Rowan, Richard Greene, and Bill Keith passing through the ranks. Fiddler Kenny Baker, who had played with him in the 1950s, also rejoined the band and remained a fixture through to the 1980s. Son James Monroe, born in 1941, also featured on bass and vocals, though he also had his own band, the Midnight Ramblers.

On August 13, 1986, one month to the day before his seventy-fifth birthday, the U.S. Senate passed a resolution recognizing his contribution to American music and culture. Bill Monroe died, age eighty-four, in 1996. Nevertheless, the music world appreciated the contribution made by the late, lamented Father of Bluegrass. As the Country Music Hall of Fame put it: "For more than half a century, Bill Monroe shaped bluegrass with his forceful mandolin playing; high, lonesome singing; and mastery of his band, the Blue Grass Boys."

BILL MONROE

BORN: September 13, 1911, in Rosine, Kentucky

DIED: September 9, 1996, in Springfield, Tennessee

INSTRUMENT: Singer, mandolin

FIRST RECORDED: 1936

INFLUENCES: Jimmie Rodgers, Arnold Shultz

RECOMMENDED LISTENING

Live Recordings: 1956–1969 (1993)

Live From Mountain Stage (1999)

The Father Of Bluegrass: The Early Years 1940–1947 (1999)

What Would You Give in Exchange for Your Soul? (2000)

The Essential (2001)

"Tubb inspired one of the most devoted fan bases of any country artist—and his fans followed him throughout his career even until the 1970s when Tubb could only croak his songs and his band was probably the least talented bunch of Troubadours. However, Tubb would 'bring the house down' every time he broke into 'Waltz Across Texas' or another favorite." From Wikipedia

purchased records by Rodgers whenever finances permitted.

In 1930, following his mother's remarriage, he went to stay with his father, who had also remarried, or with one or other of his siblings. 1933 found him working on the local roads as a laborer, where he met Merwyn "Buff" Buffington, a guitarist, who heard and approved of Tubb's singing, but suggested he should accompany himself on guitar. Tubb found a guitar in a pawn shop in Abilene, and Buffington taught him how to play the instrument. This was only a few months before Rodgers, who, astutely and with notable originality, had combined twelve-bar blues with yodeling, died of a hemorrhage. Understandably, Tubb was extremely upset by his idol's death, though according to some sources, the death of Rodgers only served to reinforce the desire to emulate his hero.

After moving to San Antonio, Tubb found that Buffington was playing guitar with two brothers on a radio station, and was persuaded to make some guest appearances, which led to a twice weekly radio show of

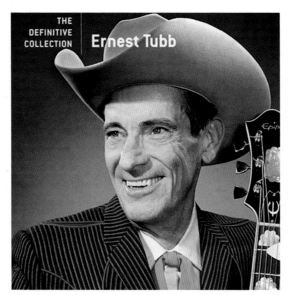

THE DEFINITIVE COLLECTION Ernest Tubb

his own. He got married in May 1934, and, still under the spell of Jimmie Rodgers, looked up the singer's widow in the local telephone directory. This led to him meeting Carrie Rodgers and persuading her to listen to his radio show. She enjoyed his singing so much that she agreed to assist him with his career, and allowed him to borrow one of her husband's guitars.

In October 1937, Tubb's mentor convinced RCA Records, for whom Rodgers had recorded, to audition him, and, soon after, his first recordings were made. However, the few tracks released at the time didn't sell. His son, Justin, who later also became a recording artist, was now two years old, and Tubb had to scrape a living during the years immediately before the Second World War. In fact, he didn't record again until 1939, this time for Decca (later MCA, now Universal), by which time he had lost the ability to yodel as his tonsils had been removed. The silver lining to this was that it helped the singer develop a style of his own rather than remaining a Jimmie Rodgers tribute act. He is believed to have later written a song with the unlikely title of "He Took Fifty Dollars and My Yodel When He Took My Tonsils Out," which proves that he had a great sense of humor as well as talent. Decca were impressed enough to persevere with him and, with sponsorship from a flour company (much like The Light Crust Doughboys), Tubb appeared on a Fort Worth radio station as the Gold Chain Troubadour.

In 1941, Tubb's first single "Walking The Floor Over You" was released. In the same year the singer also appeared in a movie, *Fighting Buckeroos*, starring Charles Starrett who made over 100 movies playing the part of the Durango Kid. The following year saw Tubb move to Nashville, and become the first honky-tonk vocalist to feature an electric guitarist on the stage of the Grand Ole Opry. When he wasn't working there, he toured, often with the flamboyant fiddle player Pee Wee King (real name Julius Frank Anthony Kuczynski), who co-wrote "The Tennessee Waltz" and was the first act to score a hit with the song, which was a Number 1 for Patti Page in 1950.

By 1944, Tubb had recruited his own band, the Texas Troubadours, whom he also began to use as backing for his recordings, including his next hit, "Try Me One More Time," which made the Top 20 of the U.S. pop chart as well as the Top 3 of the country chart. Four months later came the double-sided pop and country hit, "Soldier's Last Letter" (Number 1 country, Top 20 pop) and "Yesterdays's Tears" (Top 5 country/Top 20 pop). 1945 brought only four country hits, including a second Number 1, "It's

Right: The famous Ernest Tubb record shop, Nashville.

the singer had by now adopted the traditional Western style of dress.

Landing a regular slot on the nationally-networked Canadian Farm Hour, he put together a group of musicians known as the Rainbow Ranch Boys and began to call himself Hank the Yodelling Ranger. The show brought him to the attention of RCA Victor's Bluebird label in Montreal and he signed a recording contract with them in 1936. A string of Canadian hits followed, including his two earliest cuts for RCA, "The Prisoned Cowboy" and "Lonesome Blue Yodel," both Hank Snow originals.

Now established as a star in his native land, America, the home of country music, beckoned. The fiercely determined Snow attempted to make some headway there during the late 1930s and throughout the '40s, but was hampered not only by the ongoing war effort, but also by RCA's puzzling refusal to release his records. In 1944, he changed his name to Hank the Singing Ranger, as his voice had lowered and yodeling was now beyond him. In its place emerged the resonant baritone that would remain consistent during the rest of his long singing career.

By the end of the decade, he had made progress in the States. An appearance at The Big D Jamboree in Dallas, Texas, in 1948, where he performed a daredevil riding act, led to a friendship with country singer Ernest Tubb who brokered Snow's debut at the Grand Ole Opry in Nashville early in 1950. This coincided with RCA's decision to release his records in the United States, finally swayed by Snow's popularity in Texas. Although he would go on to become a regular at the venue and eventually relocate to Nashville, his first performance at the Opry was not well received. Furthermore, his first American single, "Marriage Vow," could only muster a solitary week on the chart, leaving a disillusioned Snow on the verge of returning to Canada.

"He was the first truly international country music star." Chas Wolfe, music historian

In the summer of 1950, however, he achieved the long-awaited breakthrough with "I'm Moving On." His next two singles "The Golden Rocket" and "The Rhumba Boogie" completed a hat-trick of chart toppers in 1951 and, between then and 1954, Snow went on to achieve an amazing twenty-four hit singles. Among these was "I Don't Hurt Anymore," which spent twenty weeks in pole position, reaffirming him as a major American star. Meanwhile, his fame was beginning to spread worldwide.

Just as Ernest Tubb had championed him, Snow lobbied the Grand Ole Opry to allow Elvis Presley, a fan of Snow's, to perform there. Presley's 1954 appearance was not an auspicious occasion; when introducing him on stage Snow forgot his protégé's name and Elvis's style was not well suited to the Opry. Nevertheless, Snow helped secure Presley's signature with RCA and also had a hand in his management, forming a booking agency with Colonel Tom Parker before being shunted aside.

In response to the rise of rock 'n' roll, Snow took a detour from his customary musical route to record some rockabilly tunes, but "Hula Rock" and "Rockin' Rollin' Ocean" were not particularly successful and he went back to a more traditional form of country. He reaped the rewards in the form of many more hits, which would ultimately amount to eighty-five entries on

Right: Snow performs in Nashville in October, 1979.

the Billboard country charts. Noteworthy songs from the era include "Big Wheels" (Number 7, 1958), "Chasin' A Rainbow" (Number 6, 1959), "Miller's Cave" (Number 9, 1960), "Beggar To A King" (Number 5, 1961), and "Ninety Miles An Hour (Down A Dead End Street)" (Number 2, 1963).

"I've Been Everywhere," a 1962 Number 1, was another of his signature songs. Snow rewrote an Australian number to incorporate a list of North American city names, which he delivered at breakneck speed. Like Hank Thompson, he was one of the first artists to create coherent albums, which often had an overall theme or concept. Snow used his skills as a guitarist to record a series of duets with "Mr. Guitar" Chet Atkins. His repertoire also included strummed ballads and fast rhumbas.

Toward the end of the '60s, Snow, like many other established country artists, found himself out of step with the new directions in which country music was heading; he was an outspoken critic of both Bakersfield pop and orchestrated country. Although his records were now less popular, he remained a major live attraction, though Snow's chart career experienced a brief but impressive renaissance in 1974 when "Hello Love" unexpectedly reached Number 1, earning him the distinction of becoming, at the time, the oldest singer to enjoy a country chart-topping single.

"I've had about 140 albums released, and I've done everything I wanted to do."
Hank Snow

The traumas of his childhood lingered in Hank's mind and, in 1976, he established his charity the Hank Snow International Foundation for Prevention of Child Abuse and Neglect of Children. During the 1950s and '60s, he entertained American troops in Korea, Vietnam, and Germany. He was inducted into the Nashville Songwriters International Hall of Fame in 1978 and into the Country Music Hall of Fame in 1979.

His legendary status was not enough to save him from being summarily dropped by RCA in 1981, however. Snow was understandably bitter about the termination of a forty-five-year association with the company, the longest continuous recording contract in the industry's history. During that time, he had assembled one of the most extensive catalogs in contemporary music—over 2,000 recordings—and released more than 140 albums. Snow has sold in excess of eighty million records and his songs have been covered by Johnny Cash, Ray Charles, Elvis Presley, the Rolling Stones, and Emmylou Harris.

Although he did not record again, Snow remained an active performer, particularly at his beloved Grand Ole Opry. Shortly after publishing his autobiography *The Hank Snow Story* in 1994, he suffered a respiratory illness but recovered to take the stage of the Opry for the final time in 1996. He died of suspected heart failure at his Rainbow Ranch home in Madison, near Nashville, on December 20, 1999.

He was survived by his wife, Minnie Aaiders, a Dutch-Irish girl whom he met in Halifax while still struggling to establish himself as a performer and married on September 2, 1935. Minnie passed away in 2003. The

"Eighty percent of today's country music is a joke and not fit to listen to." Hank Snow in 1981

couple had one son, Jimmie Rodgers Snow, born in 1936, who followed his father's footsteps by becoming a singer, also signed to RCA, but who later forsook a career in show business to become a preacher, known as Jimmy Snow.

Although one of Hank's proudest moments was becoming a naturalized American citizen in 1958, he retained many links with Canada, visiting and touring regularly. In 1997, the Hank Snow Country Music Centre was established in Nova Scotia. He was immensely proud of his Canadian heritage and Snow's status as his native land's greatest country music exponent is assured.

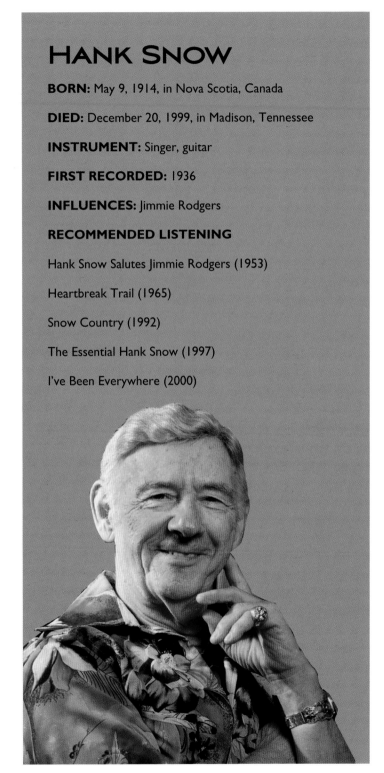

HANK SNOW

BORN: May 9, 1914, in Nova Scotia, Canada

DIED: December 20, 1999, in Madison, Tennessee

INSTRUMENT: Singer, guitar

FIRST RECORDED: 1936

INFLUENCES: Jimmie Rodgers

RECOMMENDED LISTENING

Hank Snow Salutes Jimmie Rodgers (1953)

Heartbreak Trail (1965)

Snow Country (1992)

The Essential Hank Snow (1997)

I've Been Everywhere (2000)

MERLE TRAVIS

"I thought it was just the coolest sound, because it sounded like a whole bunch of instruments coming from one guitar. In it, I heard rhythm parts, I heard melodies, I heard chords, and all this wrapped up in one." Merle Travis's son Thom Bresh

Music owes Merle Travis much, not least his foresight in commissioning the first solid-body post-war electric guitar, which paved the way for Fender's classic designs. He was equally influential in playing terms; his patented style of "Travis picking" being widely emulated over the years. He also left us some notable recordings, such as "Nine Pound Hammer," "Sixteen Tons," "Dark As A Dungeon," and "Way Down In the Mine." The latter was quite appropriate as Muhlenberg County in Kentucky, where he was brought up, is one big coalmine. Every able-bodied male in town ended up working down the mine at sometime in their lives.

Merle Travis was a major influence on the more famous Chet Atkins, his guitar style featuring complex bass-note picking. Doc Watson, another guitar giant, named his own son Merle in the hope some of his talent would rub off. Atkins explained the difference between his and Travis's styles thus: "While I play alternate bass strings which sounds more like a stride piano style, Merle played two bass strings simultaneously on the one and three beats, producing a more exciting solo rhythm, in my opinion. It was somewhat reminiscent of the great old black players."

Left: A portrait of guitar legend Merle Travis.

Travis himself was greatly influenced by Ike Everly, Don and Phil's father, who was a neighbor, and also by Mose Rager, a guitar player from Muhlenberg County. He was a coal miner who went on the road with a band of local musicians in the 1920s but didn't like it. Instead, he became a barber, but carried on doing gigs in his hometown of Drakesborough, Kentucky. Merle Travis said that he used to go to Mose Rager gigs to hear his terrific picking.

Travis's style involved damping the bass strings with the heel of his hand as he strummed, giving the playing a distinctive choked sound. He played the bass string with his thumb while using a flat pick on the upper strings.

"His highly intricate and complex guitar style, among the most accomplished in country music, was nevertheless derived from folk sources in western Kentucky, particularly from such home-grown talent as Mose Rager, Ike Everly, and Arnold Shultz." Historian Bill C. Malone

Merle Travis (born Merle Robert Travis on November 29, 1917) was the son of a tobacco farmer-turned-coalminer who was also a five-string banjo player and picked up some of his father's skills, learning the two-finger picking style common in the upper South in the 1920s and '30s. Merle, however, developed an interest in the guitar and his brother built him his first instrument. Transferring his picking technique to the larger instrument, the teenager hitchhiked around America, busking on street corners. In Indiana, he played outside a local radio station and was invited to play "Tiger Rag" on air. This got him a gig with local band the Tennessee Tomcats for the sum of thirty-five cents a day—not bad for a sixteen-year-old.

In 1937, noted fiddler Clayton McMichen invited him to join his Georgia Wildcats. A number of other groups followed, including the Drifting Pioneers, a Chicago-area gospel quartet that moved to WLW radio in Cincinnati, the major country music station north of Nashville. Here he joined forces with old-style banjo performer Grandpa Jones and the Delmore Brothers on popular radio program Boone Valley Jamboree. The group was known as the Brown's Ferry Four, while in 1943 Syd Nathan recorded Travis and Jones as "The Sheppard Brothers," the first artists for his Cincinnati-based King Records which would go on to become a leading R&B imprint.

Left: Travis photographed in 1961.

Travis spent a short stint in the Marines, but was quickly discharged and returned to Cincinnati. He left there in 1944 bound for Hollywood, where he became even more renowned, working in a variety of country bands and even launching an acting career with roles in Westerns like *The Old Texas Trail* (1944) and *Beyond The Pecos* (1945). But it was when country star Tex Ritter took him under his wing after the Second World War that Travis began amassing a song catalog. Early tracks included hits like "Cincinnati Lou," "No Vacancy," "Divorce Me COD," "Sweet Temptation," "So Round, So Firm, So Fully Packed," and "Three Times Seven." Not all featured his distinctive picking, however.

At one point, Travis occupied five out of the top six positions on the country music charts, and he also co-wrote a million-selling single—"Smoke, Smoke That Cigarette"—with writing partner Cliff Stone for his friend Tex Williams. In 1947, Travis acknowledged his musical roots with an album called *Folksongs From The Hills*. The record, which was intended to compete with Burl Ives' successful folk recordings, was released as a set of four 78rpm discs and was a failure at the time. It wasn't transferred to long-playing disc until nearly ten years later, yet contained his two most enduring songs, both describing the lives of coal miners: "Sixteen Tons" and "Dark As A Dungeon." The former was taken to the charts by Tennessee Ernie Ford, while the latter has been covered by many artists including Johnny Cash (on his best-selling concert album *At Folsom Prison*) and Dolly Parton.

At the end of the war Travis had a California steel guitar builder named Paul Bigsby make his own design for a solid-body electric instrument, with a single row of tuners that would point the way for the electric guitar as we know it today. Its design was dictated by Travis's style, which was more rhythmic and percussive than the ringing, sustained sound favored by most acoustic players. The Travis-Bigsby guitar now resides in the Country Music Hall of Fame Museum.

Above: Travis goes to Hollywood. This photo dates to 1947.

The remainder of Travis's career would be spent mostly in California, and he found his greatest success singing western and honky-tonk songs. He appeared on West Coast country television shows and featured as a guitar-picking soldier in the classic 1953 World War II film *From Here To Eternity*—a picture that starred Montgomery Clift, Burt Lancaster, Frank Sinatra, and Deborah Kerr-singing "Re-enlistment Blues."

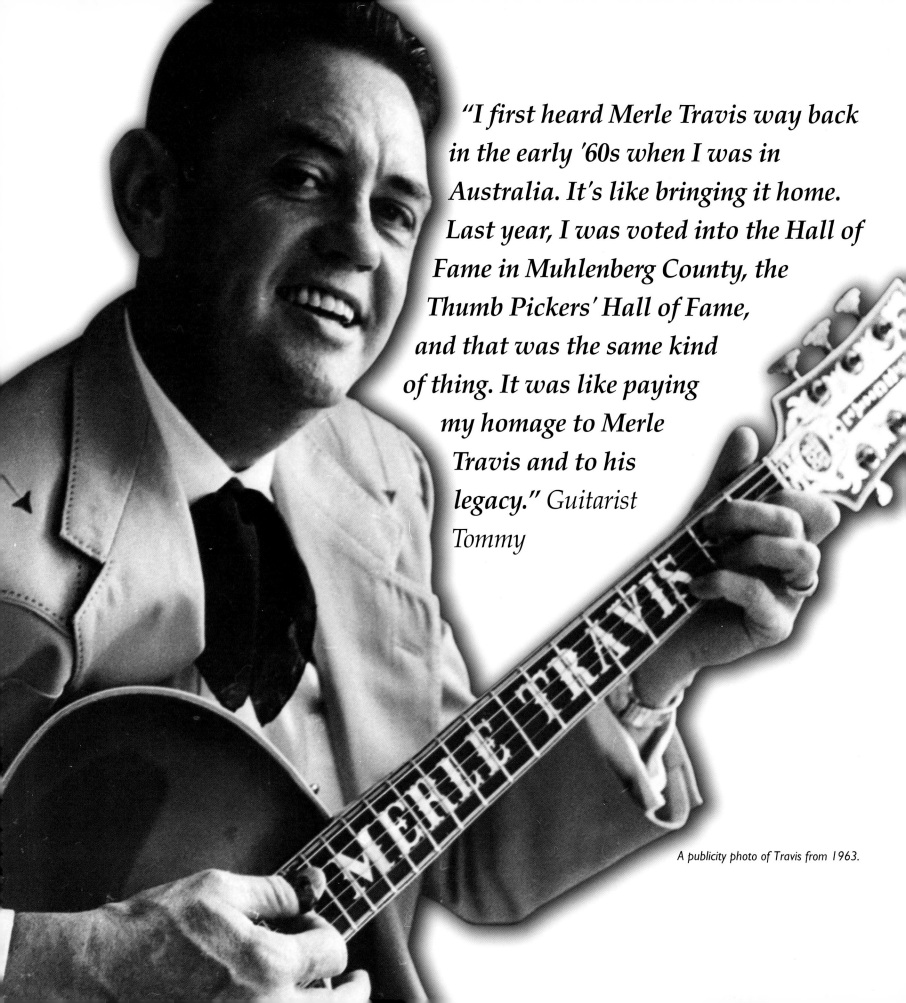

"I first heard Merle Travis way back in the early '60s when I was in Australia. It's like bringing it home. Last year, I was voted into the Hall of Fame in Muhlenberg County, the Thumb Pickers' Hall of Fame, and that was the same kind of thing. It was like paying my homage to Merle Travis and to his legacy." Guitarist Tommy

A publicity photo of Travis from 1963.

But it was his guitar playing that made Travis the stuff of legend. The 1950s and '60s saw him make a good living as a session man for hire, and though he would never regain the profile he'd enjoyed during the 1940s he remained hugely influential. At one point Travis toured and recorded as lead guitarist with Hank Thompson, who learned how to pick Travis-style and had Gibson design him a Super 400 hollow body electric guitar identical to the one Travis had used since 1952.

Off stage though, Merle Travis battled drink and drugs problems throughout this period, managing to pull his professional life together in the mid-1960s to make one new folk-style album, *Songs Of The Coal Mines*, which, like its predecessor *Folk Songs Of The Hills*, failed to sell on its original release. It would be instrumental albums such as *Walkin' The Strings* that would prove more significant and influential as must-buys for aspiring guitarists.

After Travis and his third wife, Bettie, moved to Nashville in 1968 he enjoyed a renaissance in the '70s when he was among the pioneers contributing to *Will The Circle Be Unbroken*, the Nitty Gritty Dirt Band's homage to country music's history. He was inducted into the Nashville Songwriters Hall of Fame in 1970 and elected to the Country Music Hall of Fame in 1977.

He also made further albums with Chet Atkins (their 1974 album of duets, *The Atkins–Travis Traveling Show*, won a Grammy award in the Best Country Instrumental category) and Joe Maphis, as well as collaborating with many of Bob Wills' musicians in a homage to Western swing. In 1979, he started recording for the Los Angeles-based traditional country label CMH, his 1981 *Travis Pickin'* LP receiving a Grammy nomination.

By this time Travis had curbed his wild image and lifestyle and seemed to settle down after marrying fourth wife, Dorothy, the former wife of his long-time friend Hank Thompson. Sadly, he died of a heart attack in 1983, aged sixty-five, but his legend and influence live on. A memorial was erected to him near Drakesboro, Kentucky.

MERLE TRAVIS

BORN: November 29, 1917, in Rosewood, Kentucky

DIED: October 20, 1983, in Tahlequah, Oklahoma

INSTRUMENT: Guitar

FIRST RECORDED: 1943

INFLUENCES: Ike Everly, Mose Rager

RECOMMENDED LISTENING

Folk Songs Of The Hills (1947)

Songs of the Coal Mines (1963)

The Best Of Merle Travis (1967)

Strictly Guitar (1968)

Merle Travis In Boston 1959 (1993)

EDDY ARNOLD

"Love songs. I'm crazy about love songs. And, you know, when you really stop and think about it, if you don't have love, you don't have anything." Eddy Arnold

Eddy Arnold's significance in the world of country music can be measured to some extent by the fact that he registered an almost unbelievable 145 hits in the country listing between 1945 and 1989. His singles have spent more time in the charts—including more time at the top—than those of any other singer in the music's history. Yet despite being a huge star in his own country, unlike many of his contemporaries he was only a minor player on the opposite side of the Atlantic. This was because massive popularity left him little time to target the U.K., and regular British tours were simply an impossibility.

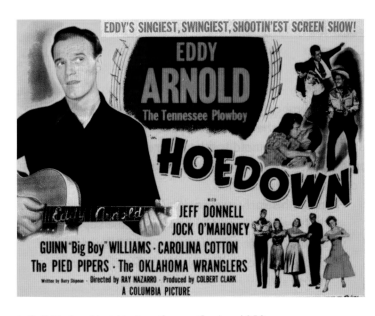

Left: Eddy Arnold at Madison Square Garden, 1959.

Richard Edward Arnold came from a large farming family in Chester County, Tennessee, and was born in on May 15, 1918, the year the First World War ended, to parents who both played instruments. As a child, he learned guitar with help from his mother and an itinerant musician, listening to records by Gene Autry, Bing Crosby, and Jimmie Rodgers on a wind-up Victrola. The death of his father before Eddy was a teenager forced him to abandon school and work on the family farm but, because they were unable to repay a loan, the property was repossessed by the bank. At this point in the Depression-ridden 1930s, Arnold abandoned farm work and decided to attempt a career in music as a vocalist. He worked on various radio stations in the Southern states before joining Pee Wee King's band, a job that took him to the Grand Ole Opry in the first half of the 1940s.

Above: Arnold and his wife Sally look over the memorabilia collection they donated to the Country Music Hall of Fame in Nashville.

made in Chicago, appeared in 1955, and The Eddy Arnold Show followed in 1956.

As well as being a pioneering country television performer, Eddy starred in the Hollywood movies *Feudin' Rhythm* (1949) and *Hoedown* (1950). He was also one of the first country artists to work the Las Vegas scene.

When singers like Elvis Presley eclipsed Arnold on the country charts, he considered retiring from the music business to focus on his interests in real estate development. Instead, he reinvented himself, dropping his plowboy image and, under the management of Gerard Purcell, began to wear tuxedos. He would henceforth be marketed as a cabaret-style singer backed by a string section and, as such, was the embodiment of hillbilly music's move from the country to the city. "When I finally put my guitar in the case the last time," he said, "I want to

be remembered just as a singer, not as a country singer or pops (sic) singer—just a singer." Reviewing an appearance he gave at Carnegie Hall in March 1968, Robert Shelton wrote in the *New York Times*: "His singing is smooth, earnest, buoyant, and uncomplicated. He is sentimental and direct. For women he seems to be a non-challenging romantic figure, and for their husbands a non-threatening man to have around the turntable."

In 1966, at the age forty-eight, Eddy Arnold was elected to the Country Music Hall of Fame. He remains the youngest inductee ever to receive the honor. In 1967, he won CMA's coveted Entertainer of the Year award, and in 1984 he received ACM's Pioneer award. In 1970, RCA hailed him for reaching the sixty million mark in lifetime record sales, a number that reportedly topped eighty million by 1985.

"I've never thought of myself as a country and western singer. With the type of material I do, I'm really a pop music artist, I want my songs to be accepted by everyone."
Eddy Arnold

Arnold announced his retirement from the stage on May 16, 1999, during a show at the Orleans Hotel in Las Vegas. He continued to record, however, and his 100th album, *After All This Time*, was released in 2005 on RCA. The National Academy of Recording Arts and Sciences inducted Arnold's recording of "Make The World Go Away" into the Grammy Hall of Fame in 1999, and the Recording Academy gave him a Lifetime Achievement Award in 2005.

Arnold's career spanned most of country music's history. Having contributed so much to that history, Arnold and his wife Sally donated their vast collection of materials documenting his career to the Country Music Hall of Fame and Museum in 2003.

Eddy Arnold died on May 8, 2008, at a care facility near Nashville. He was eighty-nine. Sally, his wife of sixty-six years, died two months earlier, and friends said privately that they didn't expect him to live long without her. The *New York Times* described him as "Eddy Arnold, the gentleman crooner who took country music uptown and sold more than eighty-five million recordings over seven decades. Mr. Arnold personified the evolution of country music in the years after World War II from a rural vernacular to an idiom with broad mainstream appeal."

EDDY ARNOLD

BORN: May 15, 1918, in Chester County, Tennessee

DIED: May 8, 2008, in Nashville, Tennessee

INSTRUMENT: Singer

FIRST RECORDED: 1944

INFLUENCES: Gene Autry, Bing Crosby

RECOMMENDED LISTENING

All Time Favourites (1956)

Cattle Call (1963)

Welcome To My World (1971)

Early Eddy Arnold (1996)

Essential (1996)

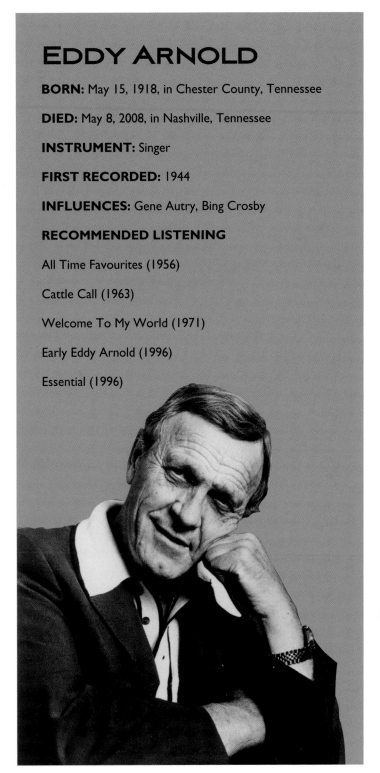

Above: Thousands file past the casket of Hank Williams.

His trademark white Stetson may have been accompanied by a flashy suit and tie, but the music retained its heartfelt appeal in Hank's hands. Nevertheless, success and its trappings seemed not to agree with a man brought up in poverty who'd sung for his supper as a kid, not to mention sold newspapers, hawked peanuts, and shone shoes. Alcohol combined with painkillers taken to combat his back problem to give Hank Williams an unwanted reputation for unreliability, a growing number of gigs being cancelled due to "indisposition."

The Opry finally lost patience with him for that reason in 1952, the same year as his marriage collapsed. Although he wed teenager Billie Jean Jones soon after, Williams was on a personal and professional downswing. He died while being driven from Knoxville, Tennessee, to Canton, Ohio, in the early hours of New Year's Day 1953. The official cause of death was a heart attack; chauffeur Charles Carr said Williams had consulted a physician before leaving Knoxville and was given two injections to help him sleep, but failed to wake up.

Hank Williams' funeral was said to have been far larger than any ever held for a citizen of Alabama and is still the largest such event ever held in Montgomery. His remains are interred at the Oakwood Annex.

Williams' legend would grow to epic proportions as the world woke to the treasury of songs he'd left behind. Death propeled his final recordings, "Your Cheatin' Heart" and the novelty "Kaw-Liga," to the top of the charts, while the canny Wesley Rose made sure his songs found homes with more mainstream performers.

Tony Bennett cut "Cold Cold Heart," Jo Stafford recorded "Jambalaya," and Frankie Laine tried "Hey Good Lookin'" for size. The story behind "Your Cheatin' Heart" was typical of the confusion surrounding the man. It was written in 1952 and was supposedly inspired by his first wife, Audrey, though inspiration came to him while driving around with his second, Billie Jean. She is supposed to have written down the lyrics for him while sitting in the passenger seat. Williams recorded the song at his last recording session in September 1952 and the song provided the title of a 1965 biopic about his life.

In 1961, Hank became one of three founder members of the Country Music Hall of Fame. The citation praised Williams' songs, which "appealed not only to the country music field but brought him great acclaim in the pop world as well." And that's certainly proved the case. Four

Above: The 1952 Cadillac in which Williams died.

"You got to have smelt a lot of mule manure before you can sing like a hillbilly." Hank Williams

decades later, an album entitled *Timeless* won a Grammy as such stellar names as Bob Dylan, Johnny Cash, Emmylou Harris, and Ryan Adams paid tribute to the "hillbilly Shakespeare." *Timeless* is well worth investigation, but more precious still is the raw, undiluted music of a man who, as his Hall of Fame citation states, "Wrote simple, beautiful melodies and straightforward, plaintive stories of life as he knew it; they will never die."

In 1987, Hank Williams posthumously received a Lifetime Achievement Grammy and was inducted into the Rock 'n' Roll Hall of Fame as a forefather of rock. Two years later came the studio-created "There's A Tear In My Beer," a duet with his son Hank Williams, Jr., which won another Grammy, while in 1994 *Life* magazine ranked Hank Williams Number 1 in its list of the 100 Most Important People in Country Music.

Not bad for a man who could neither read nor write music, but whose legacy contains more than its fair share of classics. "A good song is a good song," he once said, "and if I'm lucky enough to write it, well…! I get more kick out of writing than I do singing. I reckon I've written a thousand songs and had over 300 published."

Many songwriters have saluted Hank Williams, these ranging from Neil Young through Tim Hardin to Leonard Cohen. The latter said: "When I wrote about Hank Williams 'A hundred floors above me in the tower of song,' it's not some kind of inverse modesty. I know where Hank Williams stands in the history of popular song. 'Your Cheatin' Heart,' songs like that, are sublime, in his own tradition, and I feel myself a very minor writer."

HANK WILLIAMS

BORN: September 17, 1923, in Mount Olive, Alabama

DIED: January 1, 1953, in West Virginia

INSTRUMENT: Singer, guitarist

FIRST RECORDED: 1946

INFLUENCES: Rufus Payne, Roy Acuff

RECOMMENDED LISTENING

The Unreleased Recordings (2008)

36 Of His Greatest Hits (1957)

Hank Williams Sings 36 More Of His Great Hits (1958)

Live At The Grand Ole Opry (1976)

In The Beginning (1968)

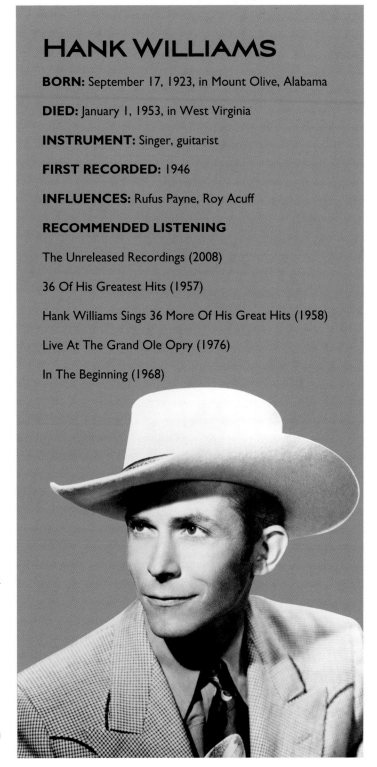

JIM REEVES

"When I was five years old, I heard my first phonograph recording. I was in the pasture, with a pet pig of mine, and was startled by the sound of music coming from the house. When I got there, there was this little suitcase on the porch, with a crank, and music was coming from it. I couldn't understand how all those people could fit inside that little suitcase." Jim Reeves

The careers of Jim Reeves, giant of country music, and Elvis Presley, the king of rock 'n' roll, have a number of fascinating parallels. Not least is the fact that, though both met an untimely end, their legends—and, most importantly, their music—have survived to enthral generations of new fans, some of whom may not even have been born in their idols' heyday.

James Travis Reeves was born in Galloway, Texas, on August 20, 1923, the youngest of a large family. Life was hard: his mother worked as a field hand after the early death of his father and money was scarce. Reeves showed his musical talent at an early age, making his first radio broadcast at age nine, four years after being given a guitar by a friend of the family. An early influence was Jimmie Rodgers, whose recordings he first heard through his older brother. From that moment on, Reeves was entranced by country music and Rodgers in particular.

He was also a talented athlete and during his teens decided to pursue a career as a baseball player. He won

Left: A publicity still of Jim Reeves, from around 1970.

an athletic scholarship to the University of Texas, but dropped out after six weeks to work at the shipyards in Houston. Soon, however, he returned to his first love of baseball, playing in the semi-professional leagues before signing with the St. Louis Cardinals and playing for them for three years. Nevertheless, he was forced to put thoughts of a professional baseball career behind after sustaining a serious ankle injury. Mary White, the school teacher he married in 1947, encouraged his musical aspirations, and as a first step to the stage he became a disc jockey at station

KWKH's
Louisiana Hayride

With a cast of more than 40 radio and recording stars including
SLIM WHITMAN
JIM REEVES
ELVIS PRESLEY
JOHNNY WALKER
JIMMY NEWMAN
and many others
3½-Hour Stage Show
and Radio Broadcast

HEART O' TEXAS
COLISEUM

TONIGHT
8:00 – 11:30 P. M.

ELVIS PRESLEY
Adults $1.90   Children 50c
Tickets on Sale At
THE COFFEE CUP
8TH AND AUSTIN

KGRI in Henderson, Texas. For a time, he was a member of Moon Mullican's band and by 1949 he was recording for a local label in Houston. Three years later, he became an announcer on country radio station KWKH, which was the home of the Louisiana Hayride, just across the Texas border in Shreveport, Louisiana.

Reeves' chances to sing were limited as a disc jockey, but everything changed one night when Hank Williams, Sr. was scheduled to appear on the Hayride, but failed to show. Reeves deputized successfully, showing few signs of nerves thanks to his experience in front of the radio microphone, and was immediately signed by Fabor Robison, the owner of Abbott Records who happened to be in the audience. "Mexican Joe" and "Bimbo" were country chart-toppers and the two most successful songs he cut for Abbott. Of the former, the ever-modest Reeves said: "nobody was as surprised as I was when it made the country hit parade and stayed there."

But it was after he appeared on the Grand Ole Opry and made the same transition as Elvis Presley by signing to RCA Victor Records that his music was heard worldwide. It was an interesting proposition: while the subject matter and instrumentation of Reeves' hits were in the honky-tonk tradition, his smooth vocal style was distinctively different from most of his peers. Some said he derived his technique from the likes of crooners Sinatra and Crosby, but there was no doubt his accessibility not only broadened his own appeal, but also that of country music as a whole. Between 1957 and 1958, he fronted his own pop radio show, fed from WSM to the ABC network. About this time, Reeves began to reshape his image as well, shifting from cowboy outfits to sport coats and slacks and even tuxedos on occasion.

With the help of RCA's Nashville chief Chet Atkins—also, of course, a gifted guitarist—Reeves was to enjoy nine years at the top of his profession. Songs like 1957's "Four Walls" typified not only his own singing style, but a

Right: Reeves in concert, 1970, now without traditional Western clothes.

new brand of smooth, laid-back country, also epitomized by the likes of Eddy Arnold and Red Foley, that would remove the "fiddles and hayseed" stigma and take country music to the wider world audience it enjoys today.

Radio-friendly Reeves chalked up a string of hits, not only in his native United States but also in Europe; Norway is still a particular stronghold. He also had a big following in South Africa where he made a movie, *Kimberley Jim*. Even if fans couldn't understand the lyrics, one journalist wrote, "the resonant purr from the honeyed larynx of Jim Reeves has an almost hypnotic effect." Reeves went on to record songs in the local language, ensuring his popularity there would continue and building a strong following in countries that had rarely been open to country music in the past.

Like Elvis, Reeves was primarily an interpretative singer rather than a songsmith and a number of major country writers profited from association with him. He also had a way with a standard. In fact, Reeves had registered nearly fifty U.S. country chart singles before a last, fatal, flight ended disastrously in July 1964. Notable successes, many of which crossed over to the *Billboard* charts, included "Four Walls" (1957), "Anna Marie" (1958), "Blue Boy" (1958), "Billy Bayou" (1959), and "Adios Amigo" (1962). His biggest U.S. pop single was 1960's "He'll Have To Go," a tale of desperation from a two-timed telephone caller, which reached Number 2 and has since found its

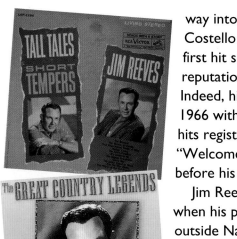

way into the repertoires of the likes of Elvis Costello and Frankie Miller. It was also his first hit single in Britain, where his reputation seemed to grow after his death. Indeed, his only U.K. chart-topper came in 1966 with "Distant Drums," sixteen more hits registering between 1964 and 1972. "Welcome To My World" was Jim's last hit before his much-mourned death.

Jim Reeves was at the height of his fame when his private Beechcraft plane crashed outside Nashville on July 31, 1964. The bodies of Reeves and his manager, Dean Manuel, were found two days later and were buried in his home state of Texas. A life-sized sculpture now stands on a one acre, tree-covered plot of ground three miles east of Carthage on U.S. Highway 79. Thousands of visitors from many countries have visited the site.

As so often happens, the artist's untimely demise brought a surge of record sales. No fewer than nine albums charted in Britain alone between August and November 1964, to add to the two Jim had already registered, ranging from the religious *God Be With You* through country themes to the seasonal *Twelve Songs Of Christmas*. Since then, Jim Reeves' legend—like Presley's—has continued to grow and his music to attract fans of new generations. Mary Reeves also kept Jim's name alive by authorizing the release of much unheard music. Most controversial were "posthumous" duets with his late country contemporary Patsy Cline (who, ironically, also died in a plane crash) and the very much alive Deborah Allen. As with Buddy Holly, new arrangements were also added to original vocal tracks to further enhance the legend. In fact, there wasn't a year between 1970 and 1984 when there wasn't a Reeves single in the charts. Although the flood of unreleased material ceased in the mid-1980s, the cult surrounding Reeves never declined, and in the '90s, Bear Family released *Welcome to My*

"Jim Reeves was the singer that Eddy Arnold wished he was." *Chet Atkins*

"The velvet style of 'Gentleman Jim' Reeves was an international influence. His rich voice bought millions of new fans to country music from every corner of the world. Although the crash of his private airplane took his life, posterity will keep his name alive because they will remember him as one of country music's most important performers."

Country Music Hall of Fame

JIM REEVES

BORN: August 20, 1923, in Galloway, Texas

DIED: July 31, 1964, in Williamson County, Tennessee

INSTRUMENT: Singer, guitar

FIRST RECORDED: 1949

INFLUENCES: Jimmie Rodgers, Moon Mullican

RECOMMENDED LISTENING

Jim Reeves Sings (1956)

Gentleman Jim (1963)

Moonlight And Roses (1964)

Distant Drums (1966)

Greatest Hits
(With Patsy Cline) (1981)

World, a sixteen-disc box set containing his entire recorded works.

The success of his back catalog and "made-in-the-studio" releases suggests that no-one has ever eclipsed "Gentleman Jim," whose memory is still rightly revered. There is a purity and simplicity to his original music that remains fresh today. He was inducted into the Country Music Hall of Fame in 1967, and two years later, the Academy of Country Music instituted the Jim Reeves Memorial Award.

HANK THOMPSON

"People only retire from things they don't like, and then they go to doing what they always wanted to do. In my case, I got into what I want to do when I got into music." Hank Thompson

In an unparalleled career that spanned seven decades, from the age of the 78rpm disc to the era of the digital download, Hank Thompson sold more than sixty million records and performed on seven continents. A true pioneer and worldwide ambassador for country music, Hank was a gifted songwriter and guitarist, blessed with a warm baritone voice that breathed life into anything he sang.

Hank Thompson was born Henry William Thompson in Waco, Texas, on September 3, 1925, the son of second generation Czech immigrants. Hank's father was a mechanic with a keen interest in electronics, which he passed on to his son, and Hank grew up listening to the country music that was ubiquitous on the radio in the area. Jimmie Rodgers and Gene Autry, "The Singing Cowboy," were among his earliest influences. The boy learned to play harmonica at an early age and this gave him a first taste of success when he consistently won a talent contest, Kiddies Matinee, broadcast on local WACO radio. The acquisition of his first guitar at ten—a Christmas

Left: Hank Thompson poses for a portrait with his guitar, circa 1960.

present from his parents—allowed him to begin to emulate his musical heroes and the precociously talented Thompson was soon starring, as "Hank the Hired Hand," in his own pre-school radio show, performing children's favorites and contemporary country tunes.

In January 1943, aged seventeen, he enlisted in the Navy, where he trained as a radio operator and technician. He continued studying electrical engineering after being discharged in March 1946, and would have pursued it as a career had music not tempted him away, though he was later able to combine the two vocations to good effect. Returning to Waco, the station declined to revive his old show and instead he was quickly snapped up by a competitor—KWTX—for a fifteen minute midday program, now styling himself simply Hank Thompson.

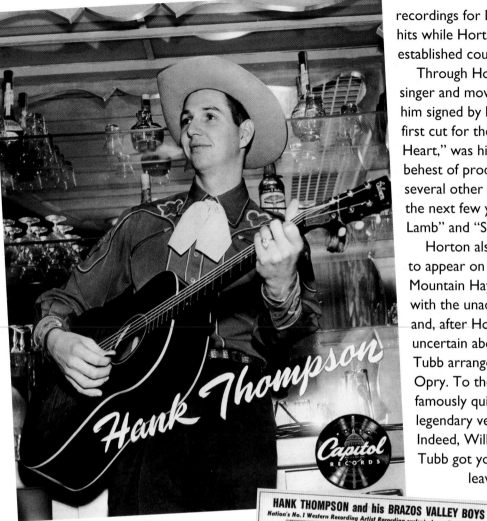

recordings for Dallas's Blue Bonnet label became local hits while Horton hustled Thompson's songs to established country stars like Ernest Tubb.

Through Horton, Hank became acquainted with singer and movie star Tex Ritter, who successfully had him signed by his label, Capitol Records. Thompson's first cut for the major label, "Humpty Dumpty Heart," was his debut national hit in 1948. At the behest of producer Lee Gillette, Thompson recorded several other nursery-rhyme inspired love songs over the next few years, including "Mary Had A Little Lamb" and "Simple Simon."

Horton also arranged for Hank to visit Nashville to appear on the Brown Brothers show Smokey Mountain Hayride. However, Thompson was uneasy with the unadventurous musical climate of the city and, after Horton died in November 1948, uncertain about continuing with the show. Instead, Tubb arranged for him to appear at the Grand Ole Opry. To the amazement of Hank Williams, Hank famously quit after his sole appearance at the legendary venue netted him a paltry nine dollars. Indeed, Williams is quoted as saying, "Man, Ernest Tubb got you on the Grand Ole Opry and you're leaving? Some of us would kill for that!"

Preferring to follow his own star, Thompson now returned to Waco, where he put together a new version of the Brazos Valley Boys with guitarist Billy Gray.

One of Thompson's problems in Nashville was that he had been unable to find musicians who could handle his take on Western swing, which combined big-band chutzpah with honky-tonk country. Thompson's hard-hitting, eminently danceable variation featured twin fiddles, steel guitar, piano, bass, and drums. In his own words, "I realized I'd never be able to play my style of music in

For live work, he put together the legendary Brazos Valley Boys in 1946, naming the band after the song "Brazos Valley Rancho." In August of that year, he recorded four songs for independent label Globe Records, including his first hit "Whoa Sailor," which he later remade for Capitol. His music began to reach a wider audience when played by DJ "Pappy" Hal Horton on his late night show on KRLD in Dallas; the well-connected Horton soon becoming Thompson's manager and mentor. Further

Above: Hank Thompson with the Brazos Valley Boys in 1967.

Nashville… They didn't allow any electric instruments. They didn't allow drums. They didn't allow horns. And where was I gonna work up there? Down in Texas I knew all these bars and honky-tonks where I could get work, because by then I was playing dance music." Nevertheless, Thompson's sound received a lukewarm reception in his native Texas, though he soon found fans in Oklahoma

City where Hank encountered manager Jim Halsey for the first time.

Thompson was a consummate showman and understood the value of a distinctive image; kitting himself out in spangled rhinestone suits, silver-toed boots, and trademark white Stetson. He did not see himself as a band leader like contemporaries Bob Wills and Lawrence Welk

Above: Thompson in front of a Capitol Records microphone in 1961.

In fact, Hank Thompson enjoyed twenty-nine chart hits in America between 1948 and 1975. In 1965, he left Capitol for a brief stint at Warner Brothers before switching to Dot Records. Session players replaced the Brazos Valley Boys as Hank adopted a more commercial Nashville sound. A traditionalist at heart, he was disillusioned by the direction country music was taking into slick Bakersfield pop. Airplay for his new work was limited and though his music drifted out of fashion, he continued recording for independent labels. Hank was rewarded for sticking to his principles in the 1980s when his kind of country music finally underwent a revival.

Above all else, Hank Williams was a pioneer, never afraid to do his own thing or take his music where others hadn't. During his spell in the navy, he began writing songs (including "Whoa Sailor") to entertain his colleagues, but his skill as a composer enabled him to embrace such diverse genres as novelty songs and romantic ballads with equal aplomb and a darker side to his songwriting was apparent when he tackled the heavy drinking and womanizing prevalent on the honky-tonk country scene. While other artists might have made such subject matter maudlin or sentimental, Hank's legendary drinking songs, notably 1965's "A Six Pack To Go," were shot through with a laid-back, often black humor.

An innovator in numerous ways, Thompson built a home studio in Oklahoma City and was one of the first artists to record in stereo. He was also at the forefront of artists making coherent albums, rather than sticking to the "hits and filler" formula, with *Dance Ranch* and *Songs For*

and eschewed the extended soloing of his rivals. Instead, Thompson favored a relaxed approach to stagecraft, chatting to fans as the band continued to play, while his background in electronics enabled him to equip the act with exciting state-of-the-art lighting and sound. Meanwhile, the Brazos Valley Boys developed as an act in their own right, cutting many instrumentals for Capitol.

One of Thompson's first recordings with new producer Ken Nelson was "The Wild Side Of Life" which, in 1952, became his first Number 1 single. Kitty Wells quickly recorded an answer song, "It Wasn't God Who Made Honky Tonk Angels." Another chart-topper, it made Wells the first female star of country music. There was nothing personal in the dueling songs though; Kitty and Hank worked together for many years. "I think mine kind of helped his record, and his helped mine," she said later.

Thompson cut an answer song of his own in 1953. "Wake Up Irene" was a response to "Goodnight Irene" an American folk standard that was a hit for the Weavers in 1950. This also marked his first collaboration with Merle Travis whose distinctive lead guitar would subsequently grace many of Thompson's recordings.

"He was one of a kind. It's a long, long legacy… his songs will last forever." D. D. Bray, Hank Thompson's manager

Rounders in the late fifties being of particular note. Hank also blazed a trail for country in Las Vegas; he and the Brazos Valley Boys recorded the first country music live album *At The Golden Nugget* there in 1961. He graduated from radio to television in the early 1950s when The Hank Thompson Show produced in Oklahoma City, was the first variety show broadcast in color.

Thompson's iconic status was reaffirmed in 1989 when he was inducted into the Country and Western Hall of Fame. He was similarly honored by the Nashville Songwriters Hall of Fame in 1997, the same year that many contemporary country stars including Lyle Lovett, Vince Gill, and George Jones paid homage by recording duets with him for the album *Hank Thompson And Friends*.

Throughout his career, Hank toured relentlessly, performing over 200 gigs per year at the height of his popularity, not just in the U.S. but all over the world, and was still playing more than a hundred dates a year when he was into his seventies, though latterly gigging was restricted to the South and Southwestern U.S. In 2000, he released an album of new material, *Seven Decades*.

Thompson was married twice. His first wedding, to long-standing girlfriend Dorothy Jean Ray, was conducted live on air during Hal Horton's radio show on April 14, 1948. After their amicable divorce, Dorothy subsequently married guitarist Merle Travis, while Thompson tied the knot with second wife Ann Williams in 1970.

A few days after canceling his Sunset Tour and announcing his retirement, Hank Thompson died aged eighty-two from lung cancer on November 6, 2007. A month previously, he performed his last concert, fittingly, in Waco on October 8, the day now proclaimed Hank Thompson Day by the city's mayor.

Hank's legacy is unmatched and his influence on country music incalculable. Reflecting with characteristic good humor on the remarkable feat of having hits in six consecutive decades, he once observed that it was "a lot easier than doing it in six non-consecutive decades."

HANK THOMPSON

BORN: September 3, 1925, in Waco, Texas

DIED: November 6, 2007, Keller, Texas

INSTRUMENT: Singer, guitar, harmonica

FIRST RECORDED: 1946

INFLUENCES: Jimmie Rodgers, Gene Autry

RECOMMENDED LISTENING

Vintage Collection (1996)

Dance Ranch (1958)

Songs For Rounders (1959)

A Six Pack To Go (1966)

At The Golden Nugget (1961)

The Best Of Hank Thompson 1966–1979 (1996)

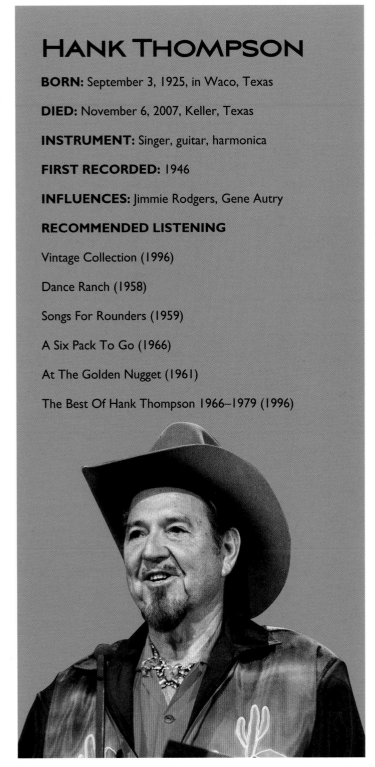

RAY PRICE

"Ray Price, who brand-marked the 4/4 bass-driven country shuffle sound of the 1950s backed by high fiddle and steel guitar, gave his sound a radical overhaul in the next decade, wrapping massed strings and harmony vocals around a pop crooning style that suggested Mario Lanza doing Porter Wagoner after a whisky-soaked boozathon in some unseemly motel dive." Mojo magazine's Andrew Male

Remaining with the same record label for over twenty years is an achievement only a few artists can claim, but country music star Ray Price is one such performer. He also accumulated well over a hundred U.S. country chart hits before 1990, an incredible achievement that very few can exceed. The few who have bettered his score include such leading lights as George Jones, Eddy Arnold, and Johnny Cash. While Price arguably never quite achieved the international fame accrued by that trio, he maintained his success for almost forty years.

Ray Noble Price was born on January 12, 1926, in Perryville, Texas, raised on a farm in Cherokee County, and—as a youngster—moved to Dallas where he learned to play the guitar. He apparently preferred the gentler rural life to the breakneck speed of urban existence. After joining the Marines for four years from 1942 he attended North Texas State Agricultural College in Abilene, but found that he could supplement his income by singing in local country clubs. This led to an appearance on Hillbilly

Left: Ray Price, photographed around 1970.

Circus on radio station KRBC in 1948, before he became a regular attraction on Big D Jamboree on station KRLD in Dallas.

By 1950, he had signed with Bullet Records, his first release a song he had also written, titled "Jealous Lies." He was friendly with Hank Williams, and after Hank's untimely demise several of Hank's Drifting Cowboys group joined Price as the Cherokee Cowboys (Price was known as the Cherokee Cowboy), though his music veered toward Western swing rather than following the musical direction taken by Williams.

After signing with CBS/Columbia in 1952, when he was also granted membership of the Grand Ole Opry, the same year brought Price his first U.S. country chart hits, "Talk To Your Heart" and "Don't Let The Stars Get In Your Eyes," which both reached the Top 5. The latter song was also a country hit for Red Foley in 1952, and for Perry Como, Gisella MacKenzie, and Eileen Barton in the 1953 U.S. pop chart.

Price would remain with CBS/Columbia until 1974, a situation that suited both label and artist. Meanwhile, the Cherokee Cowboys became a nursery for up and coming Nashville stars during the late 1950s and early '60s. Among those who were part of the group around that time were Roger Miller, who wrote Price's 1958 country Top 3 hit, "Invitation To The Blues," Willie Nelson, who wrote Price's 1963 country hit, "Night Life," Johnny Bush, and Johnny Paycheck.

A recent country music encyclopedia credits Price with giving "honky-tonk a new level of musical sophistication and a distinct musical signature that in large part persists to this day." Certainly the list of his hits includes numerous songs familiar to many pop music fans around the world, such as "Release Me," a 1954 U.S. country Top 10 hit for Price that was revived in 1967 by British balladeer Engelbert Humperdinck and topped the U.S. chart for six weeks, or his 1956 country chart-topper, "Crazy Arms."

Other Price hits include 1959's "Heartaches By The Number"—the Guy Mitchell version of this Harlan Howard composition topped the U.S. pop chart, while Price's country version made the Top 3. "Make The World Go Away" was a 1965 U.S. Number 1 for Eddy Arnold, but Price had made the Top 3 of the U.S. country chart two years earlier with his own version. In 1967, Price made the country Top 10 yet again with the well-known Irish song, "Danny Boy," his only mid-'60s country hit to cross over to the U.S. pop chart, while his biggest

"Ray Price created an era." Steel guitarist Don Helms, a veteran of Hank Williams' Drifting Cowboys

1968 country hit was "She Wears My Ring." Wikipedia also notes that "During the '60s, Price experimented increasingly with the Nashville sound, singing slow ballads and utilizing lush arrangements of strings and backing singers. This stylistic shift gained Price some success as a mainstream pop artist, although he lost appeal to many of his more traditionalist audience."

More hits followed. 1970 brought a U.S. country chart-topper with Kris Kristofferson's "For The Good Times," described as "a more mellow Price backed up by sophisticated musical sounds, quite the opposite from the honky tonk sounds he pioneered two decades before," and 1973 another country Number 1 with a version of the Jim Weatherley song, "You're The Best Thing That's Happened To Me." Price had two more Number 1 country hits in the 1970s, "I Won't Mention It Again" and "She's Got To Be A Saint." His final U.S. country Top 10 hit was "Diamonds In The Stars" in early 1982, though he continued to place songs on the U.S. country chart until the end of that decade.

In 1983, Price contributed to the soundtrack of the Clint Eastwood movie *Honkytonk Man*. *All Movie Guide* tells us "A number of Nashville legends appear in cameo roles, including Marty Robbins, Porter Wagoner, Ray Price, Merle Travis, and Johnny Gimble." The movie gave Price a

Right: The chart-topping Ray Price in concert, 1970.

Above: Ray Price at the annual Willie Nelson Fourth of July concert at the Verizon Wireless Amphitheater, 2008.

U.S. country hit with a double-sided single of "One Fiddle, Two Fiddle" and the Bob Wills classic, "San Antonio Rose." This followed his 1980 hit version of another famous Bob Wills hit, "Faded Love."

Following his appearance in the movie, Price's next hit was a plea to Willie Nelson titled "Willie, Write Me A Song," which provides substance to a possibly apocryphal story concerning Price's relationship with Nelson prior to the *San Antonio Rose* album and its hit single, "Faded Love." Apparently, the two country stars had been involved in a feud for many years, since the time they were near neighbors. One of Price's fighting roosters had killed several of Nelson's hens, so Nelson shot—and ate—one of Price's fighting cocks. Price swore he would never record another Willie Nelson song and didn't for several years, but when his old boss eventually asked him for help Nelson was pleased to oblige.

"By the early '60s, he had begun to move into a more pop-oriented direction. This trend culminated with his 1967 hit "Danny Boy." Recorded with full orchestration, the song alienated many of Price's old fans, even as it brought many new ones in from a different direction." Country Music Hall Of Fame website

RAY PRICE

BORN: January 12, 1926, in Perryville, Texas

INSTRUMENT: Singer, guitar, bandleader

FIRST RECORDED: 1950

INFLUENCES: Hank Williams, Sr.

RECOMMENDED LISTENING

For The Good Times (1970)

Ray Price's All-Time Greatest Hits (1972)

San Antonio Rose (Willie Nelson & Ray Price) (1980)

The Essential Ray Price 1951-1962 (1991)

Last Of The Breed (Willie Nelson, Ray Price & Merle Haggard) (2007)

More recently, Price has been singing gospel music and recording songs like "Amazing Grace," "Farther Along," and "Rock Of Ages," and he was still performing in nationwide country music concerts in 2006. As recently as 2007, the veteran star cut an album titled *Last Of The Breed* with Willie Nelson and Merle Haggard, which the three country veterans promoted with a two week U.S. tour.

During his lengthy career, Ray Price released nine albums that crossed over to the U.S. Top 200 album chart between 1967 and 1980, including three which were certified gold—1970's *For The Good Times*, 1972's *Ray Price's All-Time Greatest Hits* and 1980's *San Antonio Rose*, on which he shared the billing with Willie Nelson.

THE STANLEY BROTHERS

"The good Lord has blessed me all through the years to be able to do this, and I believe he'll be the man to tell me when to quit." Ralph Stanley

If country music is a specialized musical genre, then bluegrass must be nothing less than a niche. Played by acoustic stringed instruments and brought to America by European immigrants, it shares the tradition with jazz of allowing instruments to alternate with the melody. Banjo, fiddle, and upright bass all feature. The music began in the dark days of the Great Depression of 1929 and offered hope that good times were around the corner. Musically, it showed the influence of blues, gospel, string-bands, Appalachian balladry, work songs, and vaudeville. The itinerant musicians who played it moved from schoolhouse show to radio barn dances and, eventually, the recording studio.

The Stanley Brothers—Carter (born August 27, 1925) and Ralph (born February 25, 1927)—rank alongside Bill Monroe and Flatt and Scruggs as granddaddies of bluegrass. They were dab hands on banjo and guitar respectively, while the combination of their tenor and baritone voices produced a high, lonesome moan that would give even the most cynical goosebumps.

The brothers hailed from Dickenson County, Virginia, in the Clinch Mountains, and they had a singing father and banjo-picking mother. The family moved to McClure, Virginia, while the boys were young so that their parents could work a small farm, but music remained a big part of

Left: Ralph Stanley tunes up at the Telluride Bluegrass Festival, 1995.

family life with early influences including the likes of the Monroe Brothers, J. Mainer's Mountaineers, and—of course—the Grand Ole Opry on local radio. Like so many musicians from that era and that region, Stanley recalls listening to The Carter Family in the early morning hours during his Virginia childhood, as they sang such songs as "Wildwood Flower" and "Keep On The Sunny Side" on XERA, the 100,000-watt station just across the Mexico border from Del Rio, Texas.

The musical brothers had early thoughts of beginning a career of their own, but these were interrupted by war

"I think (O Brother) did well because of the old time music. There's probably thousands and thousands of people that hadn't ever heard this type of music before, and when they heard it, they liked it." Ralph Stanley

service. Carter was discharged before Ralph and, when he returned to the state, he got a job singing in Roy Sykes' Blue Ridge Mountain Boys. He quit the group as soon as Ralph returned from the Army in October of 1946 and the pair immediately formed a band, the Clinch Mountain Boys. Lead vocalist Carter was now twenty-one and tenor vocalist and banjo player Ralph, nineteen.

Using traditional Appalachian folk forms, the Stanleys created an original and memorable songbook. Indeed, Ralph used the expression "old-time, mountain style music" to differentiate the Stanleys' sound from mainstream bluegrass. After two months at the local WNVA radio station in Norton, Virginia, they went to WCYB in Bristol and soon attained popularity on the Farm and Fun Time program. They also started their recording career with Rich-R-Tone in Johnson City, Tennessee, in 1947 and signed for Columbia the following year. For the next three years, they stayed with the label, producing twenty-two songs during this stint that would

become bluegrass classics. Ralph harmonized with mandolinist Darrell "Pee Wee" Lambert on such poignant songs as "A Vision Of Mother," "The White Dove," "The Drunkard's Hell," "The Fields Have Turned Brown," "The Lonesome River," and "A Life of Sorrow." Even when the tempos were jaunty—as on classics such as "Little Glass Of Wine," "Man Of Constant Sorrow," and the banjo-fueled "Pretty Polly"—the subjects remained deep and dark.

Carter joined forces with Bill Monroe in the summer of 1951, with Ralph also playing several shows when Monroe's regular banjo player was unavailable, but while returning from one such engagement in August, Ralph was involved in a serious auto accident. Happily, he recovered and the brothers were able to relaunch the Clinch Mountain Boys. They added an innovative touch to their traditional sound in 1952 with the guitar solos of George Shuffler who often used a crosspicking style.

In the summer of 1953, they left Columbia for Mercury Records and during the mid-'50s, they made a series of recordings that expanded their boundaries as they played gospel, honky-tonk, instrumentals, and a number of original songs. However, bluegrass music grew less popular in the late 1950s and the Stanley Brothers moved to Live Oak, Florida, to headline the weekly Suwannee River Jamboree radio show on WNER, a three-hour show that was also syndicated across the Southeast. The Brothers also left Mercury at the end of the decade, and signed to Starday/King.

For about four years they played TV shows for Jim Walter Homes throughout Florida, Georgia, and Alabama while recording extensively for King, but after 1961 began to experience difficult times as opportunities for a hardcore bluegrass group waned further. They were unable to keep a full band on the road, but performed together until Carter's apparently alcohol-hastened death in 1966 at only forty-one years of age. "I think he was the

Right: Ralph Stanley and the Clinch Mountain Boys, 1998.

GEORGE JONES

"George is sick and badly needs help. Many of my friends in the music business have tried to help him over the last several weeks. It is painful for me to endure this, but my real concern is that George get some help to protect him against his own worst enemy—himself." Tammy Wynette, 1975

George Jones is widely regarded as one of the greatest, if not the all-time greatest, country vocalist, though some feel that his private life, including four marriages as well as drug and alcohol addiction, have somewhat detracted from the status of his unique vocal talent.

George Glenn Jones was born on September 12, 1931, in Saratoga, Texas, and started making hit records in 1955. His last hit (at the time of writing) was a version of the Willie Nelson classic "Funny How Time Slips Away," and came in 2006. During that half century of music-making, Jones has also made headlines for all the wrong reasons, notably because of his penchant for drugs and alcohol, though by all accounts the latter problems have been cured with the help of current wife, Nancy Sepulveda.

From a religious family background on his mother's side, George was exposed to music at an early age from both his parents' record collection and the gospel music he heard in church. When the Jones family acquired a radio in 1938 their young son became an avid listener of country music and, given a guitar two years later, was soon busking on the streets of Beaumont, Texas, where he lived.

He left home at sixteen and was soon playing guitar with a duo known as Eddie & Pearl in 1947, meeting Hank Williams at one of their shows. He then worked singing and playing on a radio station in nearby Jasper, Texas, and in 1950 wed his first wife, though this marriage was to be short-lived. Soon after, Jones became a U.S. Marine, and was based in California, somehow avoiding active service in the then current Korean war.

After serving Uncle Sam, he was discovered in 1954 by Harold "Pappy" Dailey, who signed and recorded him for

Left: George Jones with wife Tammy Wynette at Nudie's in 1973.

the Dallas-based label, Starday Records, which Dailey co-owned. Jones first made the U.S. country chart in 1955 with "Why Baby Why," and after a few more hits on Starday, signed to the larger Mercury Records. Dailey remained as his producer though, and this arrangement brought Jones his first Number 1 in 1959.

This was "White Lightning," written by J.P. Richardson, better known as the "Big Bopper" (according to *Billboard's U.S. Top Pop Singles*, Jones and the Big Bopper were also responsible for background "Indian sounds" on Johnny Preston's million-selling U.S. and U.K. chart-topper, "Running Bear"). "White Lightning" also made the Top 75 of the U.S. Top 100 pop chart to become the biggest of the five crossover hits Jones managed, a remarkably small number considering that he has amassed over 150 country chart hits. His only other two pop hits of note were two 1965 duets with Gene Pitney, one of which, "I've Got Five Dollars And It's Saturday Night," also

"Jones has mellowed into one of country music's distinguished elder statesmen." The Definitive Encyclopedia Of Country Music

"Jones is the greatest of honky tonk singers, but he has also been a victim to its lifestyle." Guinness Who's Who Of Country Music

made the Top 20 of the country chart. By then, Jones had changed labels twice. From 1962–64, he was with United Artists, after which he moved to Musicor, where he remained until 1971. In 1961, while still with Mercury, his second country chart-topper was "Tender Years," and in 1962, "She Thinks I Still Care" became his third. The contrasting styles of "White Lightning" (rockabilly) and "She Thinks I Still Care," a stately country ballad, show that Jones (and Dailey) were happy to experiment.

In 1969 Jones married his third wife, Tammy Wynette—herself a country star with three Number 1s already to her credit. Ironically, shortly after they were married, Wynette had two of her biggest hits with "D-I-V-O-R-C-E," and "Stand By Your Man," which topped the U.K. singles chart and made the Top 20 of the U.S. pop chart. It was inevitable that Mr. and Mrs. Jones would record together and, under the guidance of songwriter/producer Billy Sherrill (who worked with them individually as well as together) beween 1971 and 1980 they charted thirteen country hits, including three Number 1s: 1973's "We're Gonna Hold On," "Golden Ring" (1976), and "Near You" (1977). About the last of these, Billy Sherrill is quoted as saying: "They really weren't speaking then. Toward the end, Jones wouldn't sing anything the same way twice for Tammy, and it was hard for her to phrase with him."

Above: George Jones performing with his guitar in an undated photo.

The inevitable divorce came in 1975, reputedly due to his alcohol and drug addiction. Tammy Wynette's autobiography tells the following tale: "About 1.00 a.m. I would wake up and look over to find he was gone. I got into the car and drove to the nearest bar ten miles away. When I pulled into the parking lot there sat our rider-mower right by the entrance. He'd driven that mower right down a main highway. He looked up and saw me and said, 'Well, fellas, here she is now. My little wife, I told you she'd come after me'." As Randall Riese noted in his book *Nashville Babylon*, "They were, much to the delight of their fans, the Liz and Dick [Taylor and Burton] of country music [but] they ended as the Sonny and Cher."

Jones first achieved Number 1s with consecutive releases in 1974–75. The earlier hit was "The Grand Tour," part-written by George Richey, who would later also marry Tammy Wynette. The song told the story of a lover who has lost and describes the memories which are jogged in each part of the erstwile family home. "The Door" was along similar lines, and was still climbing the chart when Jones walked out on Wynette. It reached the top four days before she filed for divorce.

Above: Jones performs at the Patriots Theater in the Trenton War Memorial, 2006.

Since his 1983 marriage to Nancy Sepulveda, George Jones has created fewer headlines for his bad behavior, and is now regarded as a living legend. It has been estimated that there have been 450 George Jones albums released in the U.S. and U.K., and that estimate was nearly twenty years ago, though many of these are obviously compilations. He has recorded for many labels, and among the artists with whom he has shared billing are Melba Montgomery, Johnny Paycheck, and Merle Haggard.

Among the numerous awards he has won are Male Vocalist Of the Year in 1962 and 1963 in both *Billboard* and Cash Box, Top Vocal Duo (with Tammy Wynette) in 1972 and 1973 in Cash Box, Grammy for Best Male Country Vocal in 1980 for "He Stopped Loving Her Today," a song that was also the Country Music Association's Song Of The Year in both 1980 and 1981, and Single Of The Year in 1980, when he was also voted Male Vocalist Of The Year. In 1992, he was elected to the

"Regarded by many as the greatest country singer of all time and admired outside country music by people as diverse as Linda Ronstadt, Elvis Costello, Emmylou Harris, and Dave Edmunds."
Penguin Encyclopedia of Popular Music

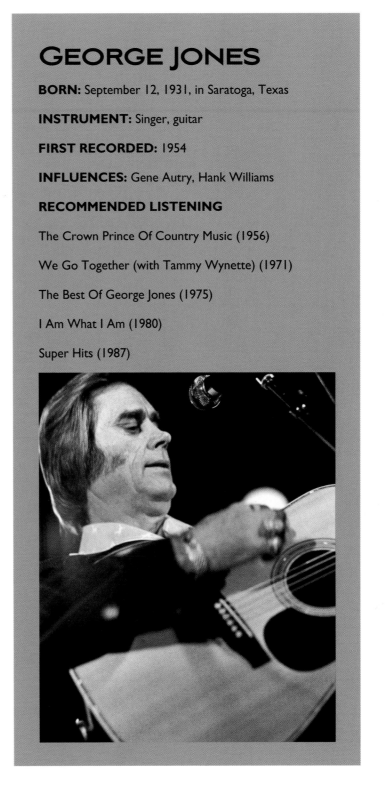

GEORGE JONES

BORN: September 12, 1931, in Saratoga, Texas

INSTRUMENT: Singer, guitar

FIRST RECORDED: 1954

INFLUENCES: Gene Autry, Hank Williams

RECOMMENDED LISTENING

The Crown Prince Of Country Music (1956)

We Go Together (with Tammy Wynette) (1971)

The Best Of George Jones (1975)

I Am What I Am (1980)

Super Hits (1987)

Country Music Hall Of Fame and in 1999 won another Grammy as Best Male Country Vocal for "Choices." "He Stopped Loving Her Today" seemed to mark a new beginning for Jones, as after that classic single was released, he returned to the top of the country charts on four occasions over the next three years, with "(I Was Country) When Country Wasn't Cool" (with Barbara Mandrell) and "Still Doin' Time" (both 1981), "Yesterday's Wine" (with Merle Haggard, 1982), and "I Always Get Lucky With You" (1983).

In 2003, Jones followed Paul Newman's footsteps by lending his name to several items of food and drink: George Jones Country Style Breakfast Sausage, George Jones White Lightning Tennessee Spring Water, and George Jones Ole Fashioned Marinades & Sauces. He also recorded his first gospel collection, which marked a reunion with producer Billy Sherrill, and received the National Medal of Arts from President George W. Bush at the White House.

PATSY CLINE

"Here was a girl, attractive but plain, simple but complicated, with a heart as big as the mountains that made her eyes shine every time she spoke of them..." Songwriter Don Hecht

It might be said that country music started as man's music, so today's female stars from Reba through Dolly to Shania owe much to the pioneering women who put in the groundwork and showed that they had as much talent as the men of Country and Western. Kitty Wells, Brenda Lee, and Loretta Lynn were three individuals who waved the flag for womanhood, but it is Patsy Cline who ranks as the first true Queen of Country. Today, her music sounds as fresh as ever and is still played and enjoyed nearly half a century after her death in a 1963 plane crash.

Born Virginia Patterson Hensley on September 8, 1932, Cline created her legend in the few short years between 1957 and early 1963—an indication of her unique talent. But she'd been a star in the making long before that, winning tap-dancing contests from the tender age of four. The gift of a piano at eight led to a place in the church choir and roles in school productions, while she proclaimed her intention of following in the footsteps of child stars Shirley Temple and Judy Garland.

When her father abandoned the family, Patsy quit school at fifteen and supported the family by playing at local dinner clubs in her hometown of Winchester, Virginia. By this time her voice had been affected by a throat

infection, resulting in a unique tone which, when allied to the expression and feeling that came with time, would make her a truly distinctive performer. Something else memorable about her were the fringed Western stage outfits she designed herself and which were made by her seamstress mother Hilda.

Patsy's early motivation was—songwriter Don Hecht later revealed—helping her mother attain the standard of life she deserved: "Patsy talked about her Blue Ridge Mountains, hunting, fishing, and about her mother. Always about her mother, and how she hurt not being able to do for her mother all he things she wanted to do. She really got me then..."

Left: A beautiful publicity shot of Patsy Cline, 1957.

Above: Patsy Cline at Nashville's Grand Old Opry.

In 1953, she married for the first time, to Gerald Cline, and, at the suggestion of her manager, changed her Christian name to Patsy—a shortened form of her middle (and mother's maiden) name. Two years later she signed to Four Star Records. Her first release, "A Church, A Courtroom And Then Goodbye," led to several appearances on the Grand Ole Opry. But none of the material recorded between 1955 and 1957—songs like "Fingerprints," "Pick Me Up (On Your Way Down)" and "A Stranger In My Arms"—were hits.

Fame finally arrived in 1957, the year of her second marriage, to Charlie Dick whom she called "the love of my life." Invited to sing on American television's Arthur

Above: Photographed in a natural setting toward the end of the '50s.

"If it had not been for people like Patsy, it wouldn't be possible for women like me to do what I do today." kd lang

Godfrey Talent Scouts show, she'd been scheduled to perform her latest single "A Poor Man's Roses (Or A Rich Man's Gold)." But the show's producers insisted she sing "Walking' After Midnight," written by Don Hecht and Alan Block. The standing ovation it won from the studio audience told its own story, and it duly found a place on her debut album.

Further hits, awards, and national acclaim soon followed, the process accelerated thanks to a recording contract with Decca Records and a link with producer Owen Bradley. She would record fifty-one tracks for Decca between 1960 and 1963, the same number she had cut for Four Star Records between 1955 and 1960. But her joy at being accepted as a member of the Grand Ole Opry was tempered when a car accident in 1961 took Patsy out of circulation and almost cost her life. Patsy and her brother Sam were involved in a head-on collision in front of Madison High School in Nashville. The impact sent her through the windshield and nearly killed her, but she survived. Due to the accident, Patsy got a visible scar on her forehead, and because of that she wore wigs at her public performances from then on.

She came back strongly, however, with crossover hits "Crazy," written by Willie Nelson, and "I Fall To Pieces," co-written by Harlan Howard and Hank Cochran, sung in what one critic called her "characteristic sad and lonesome vocal sound." In fact, Cline had claimed that "Crazy" was too difficult to sing because the high notes pained her injured ribs from the car accident, but she actually recorded the song in one take. Her version,

Above: A sophisticated Cline swaps her own designs for cocktail dresses.

which was completely different to Nelson's demo, turned out to be both a classic and, ultimately, Cline's signature song. Loretta Lynn later reported that the night Cline premiered "Crazy" at the Grand Ole Opry, she received three standing ovations.

Her brief, two-year hitmaking career continued with "When I Get Through With You" and "Leaving On Your Mind." To match her new, sophisticated sound, Cline swapped her Western trademark cowgirl outfits for designer gowns, cocktail dresses, high heels, and even gold lame pants. This challenged the then-conservative country music industry but, like her sound, Cline's style was to prove influential.

Her success inspired others too. Believing that there was "room enough for everybody," and confident of her abilities and appeal, Cline encouraged a number of women starting out in music, including Loretta Lynn, Dottie West, Barbara Mandrell (with whom Cline once toured), Jan Howard, and Brenda Lee. All cite her as an influence in their careers. She came to meet Loretta Lynn for the first time after she heard her singing "I Fall To Pieces" in a radio broadcast from Ernest Tubb's record shop after her accident. Patsy sent husband Charlie to fetch Loretta and bring her to the hospital—it was the beginning of a special friendship.

Indeed, many of Patsy Cline's current fans were first introduced to her music in Loretta Lynn's autobiography, *Coal Miner's Daughter*, and in particular the movie that was made of the book in 1980, which featured Beverly D'Angelo as Patsy.

Patsy Cline was not to live to enjoy her success. Her story ended on March 5, 1963, when the plane bringing her and fellow stars Cowboy Copas, Hawkshaw Hawkins, and Randy Hughes home from a benefit concert in Kansas City fell to earth three miles west of Camden, Tennessee. She was just thirty years of age. Nevertheless, the music she left behind will ensure Patsy's name lives on. She was the first female solo singer to be elected to the Country Music Hall of Fame in 1973, while *Sweet Dreams*, a biopic

"Her heritage of timeless recordings is testimony to her artistic capacity." Country *Music Hall of Fame plaque*

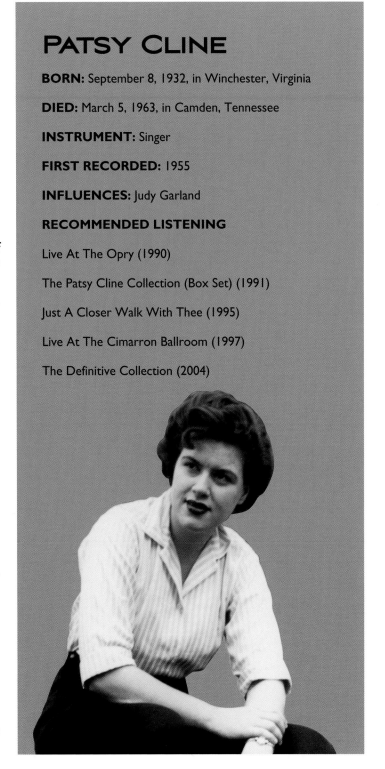

PATSY CLINE

BORN: September 8, 1932, in Winchester, Virginia

DIED: March 5, 1963, in Camden, Tennessee

INSTRUMENT: Singer

FIRST RECORDED: 1955

INFLUENCES: Judy Garland

RECOMMENDED LISTENING

Live At The Opry (1990)

The Patsy Cline Collection (Box Set) (1991)

Just A Closer Walk With Thee (1995)

Live At The Cimarron Ballroom (1997)

The Definitive Collection (2004)

starring Jessica Lange, was released in 1985. A Lifetime Achievement Grammy also came in 1995.

Patsy's producer, Owen Bradley, came out of retirement to work with kd lang after hearing her cover of "Three Cigarettes In An Ashtray"—and Lang is just one of many country singers, most recently LeAnn Rimes and American Idol's Carrie Underwood, to acknowledge Patsy Cline's enduring influence. As guitarist Harold Bradley, brother of Owen, once said, "She's taken the standards for being a country vocalist and raised the bar. Women, even now, are trying to get to that bar."

In 1981, "Have You Ever Been Lonely (Have You Ever Been Blue)," an electronically produced duet between Cline and Jim Reeves, another legendary singer who died the year after Patsy in similar circumstances, was a Number 5 country hit. Two decades later, she was voted by artists and members of the Country Music industry as Number 1 on CMT's television special of the Forty Greatest Women of Country Music of all time. In 1999, she had been voted Number 11 on VH1's special The 100 Greatest Women in Rock 'n' Roll.

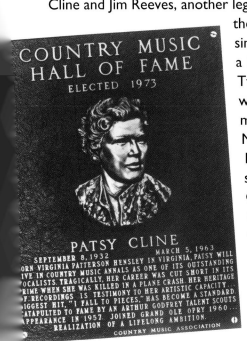

25 inches

12½ in. long

34 - D

38 cm.

Shoulders 14½ in.

skirt 27½ cm

waist to bottom

JOHNNY CASH

"You build on failure. You use it as a stepping stone. Close the door on the past. You don't try to forget the mistakes, but you don't dwell on it. You don't let it have any of your energy, or any of your time, or any of your space." Johnny Cash

Johnny Cash, the self-styled "Man In Black," has transcended country music to become a popular music icon. He was one of the most influential musicians of the Twentieth Century, selling over ninety million albums in his near fifty-year career. His distinctive baritone, "scrubbing" guitar style, and the mixture of wry humor and pathos in his songs made him unique not only in country but music as a whole.

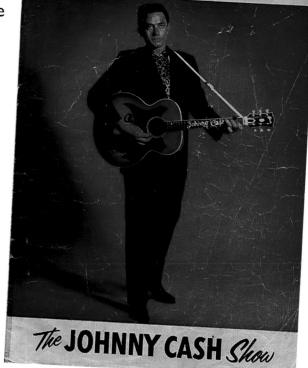

Born on February 26, 1932, the young Cash worked as a child on the family farm in Arkansas and was much affected by the death in a machinery accident of elder brother Jack. His first musical influences came from the radio and he imbibed a wide variety of music while growing up in the 1930s and '40s—sentimental old-time ballads, traditional country, blues, and gospel—that would find expression in his own output. In fact, Cash began writing songs at an early age after being given a guitar. He performed national service in the U.S. Air Force before being discharged in 1954 and took up the guitar seriously while stationed in Germany. On his return home Cash took a job as an electrical appliance salesman, but

Left: A publicity still of Johnny Cash dating to 1956.

approached Sun Records' Sam Phillips in 1955 asking for a chance to record with guitarist Luther Perkins and bassist Marshall Grant (known as the Tennessee Two). Signing to Sun, he became a labelmate of Elvis Presley, Roy Orbison, Carl Perkins, and Jerry Lee Lewis.

"I Walk The Line," released by Sun in 1956, remains his best known song. It was also Cash's first major hit and provided the title of the 2005 biopic *Walk the Line* as well

"How well I have learned that there is no fence to sit on between heaven and hell. There is a deep, wide gulf, a chasm, and in that chasm is no place for any man." Johnny Cash

Bob Dylan, with whom Cash sang a duet on his 1969 country album *Nashville Skyline* and for which he wrote the album's liner notes, called Johnny "America's greatest living storyteller," while Cash himself, tongue firmly in cheek, summed up his appeal thus: "I don't dance or wear my pants too tight… but I do know about a thousand songs!"

From 1969 to 1971, Cash starred in his own television show, The Johnny Cash Show, on the ABC network. He played the White House in 1972 and rubbed shoulders with every president from Nixon onward, while in the '80s he cut a series of albums with country "outlaws" like Kris Kristofferson, Willie Nelson, and Waylon Jennings. His recording career then stagnated, however, until, in 1994, he began a series of albums called American Recordings with metal/rap producer Rick Rubin. These were named after the record label he was then signed to, but there's little doubt that the man distilled into them all that was great about his country's music. And this was soon to be realized by another generation. Cash went on to collaborate with U2 and also covered "Hurt," a song by Nine Inch Nails. His second *American Recordings* album, *Unchained*, released in 1996, won a Grammy.

It was during a performance in October 1997 in Flint, Michigan, that Cash first revealed he was fighting a form of Parkinson's disease. He dropped the bombshell after nearly falling over trying to retrieve a guitar pick, and insisted bravely that "It's all right. I refuse to give it some ground in my life." The inevitable headlines that ensued cast an understandable shadow over the final years of

Left: The "Million Dollar Quartet" in 1956. Cash stands behind Presley.

Above: Cash puts on a show for inmates at Cummins Prison, 1969.

181

Cash's life, though he managed to make a few live appearances and record two more albums. "I've had forty-three years of touring," he told Rolling Stone magazine, "That's enough. I can direct my energies more to recording now. I intend to keep recording as long as I'm able. It's what I do. It's what I feel."

The diagnosis was eventually modified to diabetes, but it was clear that, as he approached seventy, Johnny Cash's public appearances would now be few and far between. One was in April 1999, at an all-star tribute show to himself starring Bob Dylan, Willie Nelson, Bruce Springsteen, Kris Kristofferson, and many more. As it happened, June predeceased her husband by four months, passing away in May 2003 at the age of seventy-three after heart surgery.

The biopic *Walk The Line*, starring Joaquin Phoenix as Johnny and Reese Witherspoon as June, was released in the United States in November 2005 to considerable critical acclaim. Both Phoenix and Witherspoon performed their own vocals in the film, while Phoenix, who learned to play guitar for the role of Johnny Cash, received the Grammy Award for his contributions to the soundtrack. John Carter Cash, the only child of Johnny and June, was an executive producer on the film.

Cash had four daughters with first wife Vivian, including singer-songwriter Rosanne: a later stepdaughter, Carlene Carter, would also find limited fame.

He was not to be the last surviving member of the so-called "Million Dollar Quartet"—Jerry Lee Lewis having outlived Cash, Elvis Presley, and Carl Perkins—but he turned out a body of music that stands comparison with any Twentieth Century artist, let alone his Sun label-mates. The fact that, in his later years, he worked with such cutting-edge talents in their own areas as producer Rick Rubin, songwriter Trent Reznor of Nine Inch Nails, and video director Anton Corbijn, a close collaborator of U2, shows he was never content to rest on past glories.

Left: A pensive portrait of Cash, 1957.

JOHNNY CASH

BORN: February 26, 1932, in Kingsland, Arkansas

DIED: September 12, 2003, in Nashville, Tennessee

INSTRUMENT: Singer, guitar

FIRST RECORDED: 1955

INFLUENCES: The Carter Family, Dennis Day

RECOMMENDED LISTENING

I Walk The Line (1964)

At Folsom Prison (1968)

At San Quentin (1969)

Original Golden Hits Volume I (1969)

American Recordings (1994)

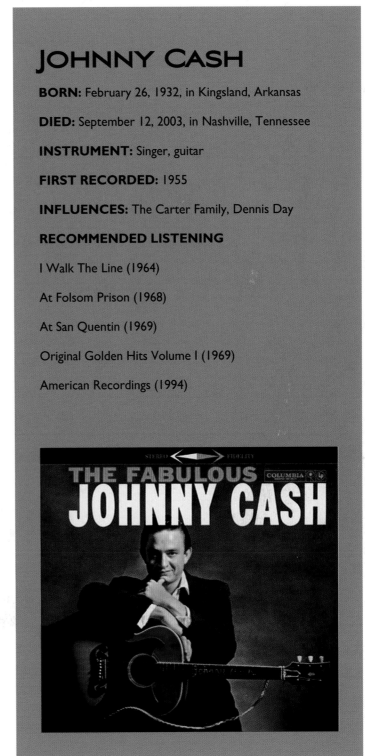

THE MUSIC ON THE CD

1. **Blue Yodel** (Rodgers) Public Domain
Jimmie Rodgers' celebrated series of Blue Yodels saw him draw from Appalachian ballads, black spirituals, rural blues and white pop music—all elements that would later feed into rock'n'roll. The Yodels are a series of thirteen songs written and recorded by Rodgers between 1927 and 1933, based on the twelve-bar blues format and featuring Rodgers' trademark vocal. The style of music came to be called "hillbilly."

2. **Wildwood Flower** (Irving/Webster, arr Carter) Peermusic (UK) Ltd
In May 1928 Ralph Peer called The Carter Family to Camden, New Jersey, for a recording session; the going rate was $75 a song. Among the titles recorded at this session was "Wildwood Flower," named by National Public Radio decades later as one of the "100 most important American musical works of the twentieth century."

3. **Night Train To Memphis** (Hughes/Bradley/Smith) Memory Lane Music Ltd/Peermusic (UK) Ltd
A hit in 1943, "Night Train To Memphis" titled a movie three years later starring Roy Acuff and his Smoky Mountain Boys. Along with "The Great Speckled Bird," it remains Acuff's best-known song today, nearly two decades after his death.

4. **Stay A Little Longer** (Wills/Duncan) Peermusic (UK) Ltd
Bob Wills has been revered by such country music legends as Merle Haggard and Willie Nelson. The latter covered Wills' "Stay A Little Longer," but the original—featured here—was recorded in 1945 and reached Number 3 in 1946.

5. **Blue Guitars** (Campbell/Reinhart) Copyright Control
Recorded in Dallas in 1937, this number featured John "Knocky" Parker on piano, Muryel Campbell on electric guitar, and Kenneth Pitts on fiddle. It was the Doughboys' second attempt at cutting "Blue Guitars," a 1936 recording from Fort Worth remaining unreleased.

6. **Red River Valley** (Trad) Public Domain
This classic cowboy lament for a lost love named a 1936 Western in which Gene Autry starred as himself. "Red River Valley" is a folk song that has gone by different names—"Cowboy Love Song," "Bright Sherman Valley," "Bright Laurel Valley," "In The Bright Mohawk Valley," and "Bright Little Valley"—while Johnny and the Hurricanes recorded a rock'n' roll adaptation, "Red River Rock," in 1959.

7. **Blue Moon Of Kentucky** (Monroe) Peermusic (UK) Ltd
Bill Monroe's late-1940s recordings for Columbia, made with Lester Flatt and Earl Scruggs, are now regarded as definitive. "Blue Moon Of Kentucky" was recorded in 1947, and it was when Elvis Presley recorded the classic song on his historic Sun session in July 1954 that bluegrass music made the mainstream for the first time.

8. **Walking The Floor Over You** (Tubb) Campbell Connelly & Co Ltd
Ernest Tubb first included the sound of a steel guitar in his recordings in 1941, which was also the year of his first million-selling single, "Walking The Floor Over You." He also performed the song in the film *Fighting Buckeroos*.

9. **I'm Moving On** (Snow) Carlin Music Corp
In the summer of 1950, Hank Snow achieved his long-awaited breakthrough in spectacular style when the first of his great traveling songs "I'm Moving On" swiftly ascended to Number 1 and remained there for a remarkable twenty-one weeks.

10. **Nine Pound Hammer** (Travis) Campbell Connelly & Co Ltd
This is one of Merle Travis' most familiar numbers and first appeared on 1947's *Folk Songs Of The Hills*, alongside originals "Sixteen Tons," "Dark As A Dungeon," and "Over By Number Nine."

11. **I'll Hold You In My Heart** (Arnold/Horton/Dilbeck) Keith Prowse Music Publishing
Eddy Arnold's "I'll Hold You In My Heart (Till I Can Hold You In My Arms)" was a major country hit. The song's crossover into the pop market paved the way for later acts like Jim Reeves to do likewise.

12. **Move It On Over** (Williams) Sony/ATV Music Publishing (UK)
Written and recorded by Hank Williams in 1947, this was his first major hit, reaching Number 4 on the *Billboard* country chart. The song is similar in its twelve-bar format to "Rock Around The Clock" which, released five years later, would be hailed as the first rock 'n' roll hit single in the hands of Bill Haley and his Comets.

13. **Four Walls** (Campbell/Moore) EMI United Partnership Ltd
For Jim Reeves, 1957's "Four Walls" was the turning point in his career, proving to both him and his producer Chet Atkins that ballads would be his main source of success. It stayed at Number 1 for eight weeks, and went to Number 11 on the pop chart at the same time. Its popularity helped usher in the "Nashville Sound" a new style of country music using violins and lush background arrangements.

14. **The Wild Side Of Life** (Warren/Carter) EMI United Partnership Ltd
One of Hank Thompson first recordings with producer Ken Nelson was "The Wild Side Of Life" which, in 1952, became his first Number 1 single. Written by Arlie Carter and Willie Warren, it utilized an old country melody to tell the tale of a woman rejecting domestic life in favor of the barroom. The song spent 15 weeks at the top of the *Billboard* country chart and sold a million copies.

15. **Crazy Arms** (Mooney/Seals) Universal/MCA Music Ltd
Ray Price's 1956 U.S. country chart-topper "Crazy Arms" has become a standard with assistance from Jerry Lee Lewis, who covered it for his debut single that same year. Price used the song to introduce fans to his Texas shuffle sound: fiddle, pedal steel guitar, walking electric bass, and a swinging four-four rhythm. These remained hallmarks of his hits before he began experimenting with strings and pop styles in the '60s.

16. **Little Maggie** (Trad, arr Stanley) Lark Music Ltd
"Little Maggie" was the flip side of the Stanley Brothers' first hit, "Little Glass Of Wine," released in March 1948, and was a solo showcase for Ralph Stanley's vocal and two-finger style banjo work. In 2007, some six decades later, Bob Dylan brought it back to the world's attention when he played it on his internationally syndicated XM radio show in a themed evening of songs titled by women's names.

17. **Slowly** (Hill/Pierce) Carlin Music Corp
Webb Pierce's first Number 1 of 1954 was "Slowly," which he co-wrote with Texas fiddler Tommy Hill. The *New Musical Express* suggested the song was a trendsetter "because of Bud Isaacs' electric pedal steel guitar, which created a style that was copied by most other country bands."

18. **Why Baby Why** (Jones/edwards) Peermusic (UK) Ltd
Produced by Starday co-founder and George Jones' manager Pappy Daily, "Why Baby Why" peaked at Number 4 on the *Billboard* country charts that year. Sales prospects were damaged by Red Sovine and Webb Pierce's Number 1 cover duet, but Jones's version was also the first track on his 1957 debut album, *Grand Ole Opry's New Star*.

19. **Walking After Midnight** (Hecht/Block) Acuff-Rose Music Ltd
The song was originally written for pop/jazz vocalist Kay Starr. However, Starr's recording company, Capitol, did not want her to record it. Co-writer Don Hecht felt Patsy Cline's voice was suited to the song, but she thought the song too pop-oriented. Invited to sing on American television's Arthur Godfrey Talent Scouts show in 1957, the show's producers insisted she sing "Walkin' After Midnight." The standing ovation it won from the studio audience told its own story.

20. **I Walk The Line** (Cash) Carlin Music Corp
"I Walk The Line," released by Sun Records in 1956, was Cash's first major hit. The song was also the source of the title of the 2005 biopic *Walk The Line* as well as a non-biographical 1970 movie starring Gregory Peck. The song is built around the "boom-chicka-boom" or "freight train" rhythm common to many of Cash's songs and originally adopted in the absence of drums.

CREDITS

FURTHER READING

Books

Illustrated Encyclopedia of Country Music; Salamander Books, 1986
The Billboard Book of Number 1 Country Hits; Guinness, 1991
The Guinness Who's Who Of Country Music; Colin Larkin, Guinness,1993
The Big Book Of Country Music; Richard Carlin, Penguin, 1995
The Country Music Encyclopaedia; Melvin Shestack, Omnibus Press, 1977
The History of Rock Partwork; Orbis, 1981-84

Websites

Country Music Television; www.cmt.com
Country Music Hall Of Fame; www.countrymusichalloffame.com
Roughstock's History of Country Music; www.roughstock.com/history
Country Music Association; www.cmaworld.com
Bluegrass World; www.bluegrassworld. com